INSIDE
MARINE ONE

Four U.S. Presidents, One Proud Marine, and the World's Most Amazing Helicopter

Colonel Ray "Frenchy" L'Heureux
with Lee Kelley

ST. MARTIN'S GRIFFIN
NEW YORK

TO MY PARENTS,

ROGER AND VIRGINIA L'HEUREUX,

AND MY CHILDREN,

RAY JR. AND DELIA

INSIDE MARINE ONE. Copyright © 2014 by Colonel Ray L'Heureux with Lee Kelley.
All rights reserved. Printed in the United States of America. For information, address
St. Martin's Press, 175 Fifth Avenue, New York, N.Y. 10010.

www.stmartins.com

Designed by Omar Chapa

The Library of Congress has cataloged the hardcover edition as follows:

L'Heureux, Ray, 1961–
    Inside Marine One : four U.S. Presidents, one proud Marine, and the world's most
amazing helicopter / Colonel Ray "Frenchy" L'Heureux with Lee Kelley.—First edition.
        p. cm.
Includes index.
ISBN 978-1-250-04144-9 (hardcover)
ISBN 978-1-4668-3775-1 (e-book)
    1. L'Heureux, Ray.   2. Marine One (Presidential aircraft)   3. United States Marine
Corps—Officers—Biography.   4. Helicopter pilots—United States—Biography.
5. Presidents—Transportation—United States.   6. Presidents—United States—
Anecdotes.   I. Kelley, Lee, 1971–   II. Title.
    TL723.L45 2014
    359.9'6092—dc23
[B]

2014008046

ISBN 978-1-250-06843-9 (trade paperback)

St. Martin's Griffin books may be purchased for educational, business, or promotional
use. For information on bulk purchases, please contact the Macmillan Corporate and
Premium Sales Department at 1-800-221-7945, extension 5442, or write to specialmarkets
@macmillan.com.

First St. Martin's Griffin Edition: July 2015

10   9   8   7   6   5   4   3   2   1

CONTENTS

INTRODUCTION

As I banked the President's helicopter to the left, I was flying only about a hundred feet above a sea of people. It was the cold and clear morning of January 20, 2009, and I was flying President George W. Bush in *Marine One*, the world's most famous helicopter. This was his "victory lap," and we were cruising over a crowd of an estimated two million people who had gathered in Washington, D.C. for President Obama's inauguration ceremony.

The view through the glass of my cockpit was better than any 3-D movie screen could ever be. It was filled with a colorful panorama of waving hands, American flags on little sticks, and smiling faces breathing puffs of frost out through their hooded winter coats and caps. The Washington Monument and the Lincoln Memorial had become more than just historical landmarks for me. I used them as reference points to maintain a good altitude and circle over the National Mall once again.

From the ground, I can only imagine what people were thinking and feeling when they turned their eyes up at *Marine One*, the President's helicopter, with UNITED STATES OF AMERICA emblazoned in white letters on each side. I swung around in a wide circle as the crowd continued to cheer and wave, and I got another spectacular view of our nation's capital draped in the traditional bright red, white, and blue bunting that is used only once every four years. At one point, I actually caught a glimpse of my own helicopter on one of the many JumboTrons set up to display the inauguration ceremonies that day.

I had been President Bush's helicopter pilot for a couple of years and I had flown him all over the planet. I had grown accustomed to carrying precious cargo. But today was different. I wasn't carrying only President Bush, the man who had been my Commander in Chief until only a few moments earlier; I was also carrying First Lady Laura Bush, their two daughters, Jenna and Barbara, Jenna's husband, Henry Hager, and their grandparents, former President George H. W. Bush and former First Lady Barbara Bush.

I knew that both former President Bushes and their families were looking down at the same sights as I was. But what were they thinking about? What did the people below us see? And what did we look like to the millions of people around the world watching us on TV? My sense of pride and patriotism swelled within me. I was both energized and humbled by the small part I was playing in this theater of living history.

I had already made a couple of laps over the crowd, trying to bide my time while Vice President Cheney made his way in a separate helicopter to Andrews Air Force Base, where he would introduce President Bush for his farewell speech to a large crowd gathered there. I was enjoying this so much that I could easily have made a hundred more laps, but this was my third lap. The boss knew how long the trip took, and I had to get my passengers to Andrews. Finally, the call came over the radio that the Vice President was almost in place.

I smiled and turned *Marine One* smoothly to the east, then made a slight turn to the right, aiming at the well-known confluence of the

Potomac and Anacostia rivers, which led into Maryland. It had been a remarkable morning, and now it was time to land President Bush one last time. As I tried to soak in every moment of the historic flight, I was still amazed that a small-town boy from New England like me could be so lucky. . . .

My name is Ray "Frenchy" L'Heureux, and I am a former Colonel in the United States Marine Corps. I received my honorable discharge in 2011, after a thirty-year career. While I had many amazing experiences, the pinnacle of my career was serving in Marine Helicopter Squadron One (HMX-1). The first and largest aviation squadron in the Marine Corps, HMX-1 employs more than seven hundred hand-selected Marines, Sailors, and civilians, including a fleet of helicopters and its complement of pilots. HMX-1 has several different missions, but the primary and most visible one is providing executive transport to the President of the United States around the clock and around the globe.

Most people are aware that *Air Force One* is the President's plane, but fewer people realize that the President also has his own helicopter support (*Marine One*). Unlike most Americans, every move the President makes is closely coordinated. In fact, the President of the United States travels in one of three ways: in his motorcade, in *Air Force One*, or in *Marine One*. *Air Force One* will take the President on long flights, but his motorcade or *Marine One* will take him on the countless shorter trips once he arrives at his destination. And since flying in a helicopter doesn't require closing down streets and impacting local traffic, over the years it has become a preferred method of travel.

The United States is the only country in the world that provides executive transport to the Commander in Chief, no matter where he travels in the world. So, whether *Air Force One* brings the President from the White House to New York City or to Europe, *Marine One* will be right there standing by when he lands.

I joined the Marine Corps during college, and then spent most of my adult life chasing and exceeding all the flying dreams and aspirations I'd had as a kid. From 1992 until 1996, I served as a young Marine Officer in HMX-1, supporting President George H. W. Bush and then President Bill Clinton, and participating in many historical operations. More recently, in 2006, I returned to HMX-1 to serve as Commanding Officer of HMX-1, assuming the duties of Presidential Helicopter Pilot for George W. Bush and then Barack Obama.

People seem to love behind-the-scenes stories of *Marine One*. I have also realized just how unique my job—my responsibility—was. Each Commanding Officer serves for only four years. I was the twenty-second out of fewer than twenty-five *Marine One* pilots in history. And since I also flew President Bush (41) and President Clinton early in my career, I may be the only Presidential Pilot in HMX-1 history to "carry" four consecutive Presidents. I am also the only Presidential Pilot to carry the last two presidents of the twentieth century and the first two of the twenty-first.

Most people see the President only through the lens of the media or news, and very few people know anything about HMX-1 or the inner workings of the green-and-white helicopter that they see landing on or taking off from the White House lawn. I'm the grateful guy who had a bird's-eye view of it all. *Marine One* has been called the world's most famous helicopter. I won't dispute that. It still astounds me to think of all the people I have flown in that aircraft. I flew four Presidents, their families, and their staffs across the United States and around the world, day and night and in every kind of weather. I've been charged with flying some of the most enigmatic and well-known leaders and personalities of our time. I've gone hiking with Pope John Paul II. I shared drinks at Normandy with WWII vets. I landed *Marine One* on the lawn of Windsor Castle, and I went mountain biking across Camp David and the ranch in Crawford with President Bush.

This is a human story, as told in human terms by an average

Marine. It is a story of a life I could not of imagined, but also one of humility, and I was privileged to have lived the story as it unfolded. I have tried to live up to the standards that were ordained for me. I think I succeeded most of the time, but not all of the time. In the end, I remain the person my parents raised me to be, and the Marine I was inspired by others to be. Always moving forward, and when knocked down, standing up the only way one can—straight and true.

Let me share my story with you. I'll take you with me on my journey through the ranks of the Marines, tell you just what it took to be selected as a member of HMX-1, how I felt when I flew those incredible machines, and how I was eventually selected as the Presidential Pilot and HMX-1 Commander. It was truly a privilege and an honor that I'd like to share with you.

Let me take you inside *Marine One*.

CHAPTER 1

A YOUNG BOY DREAMS OF FLYING

Daydreamer

I was born in Salem, Massachusetts on July 24, 1961. A couple of years before that, my parents bought a three-story, sixteen-room, old Greek Revival–style house in historic Salem, about fifteen miles north of Boston. My dad was an electrical engineer. My mom was a devoted, hardworking homemaker, and they planned to fill the place with kids. That agenda seemed to work out perfectly, because I am the third of seven siblings. My sister Yvonne and my brother Roger are older than I. My sister Marilyn was born next, followed by my three brothers, Marc, Tommy, and Paul.

The house was built in the mid-1800s, and I imagine my parents must have thought that its location and size outweighed its age and impracticality. The style resembled a miniature Parthenon—a mint-green box with white trim and a peaked roof. For a long time, my sisters shared a room, Roger and I shared a room, and the three younger brothers shared another one. As we got older, we spread out into our own spaces, but in the early years my parents consolidated all of us kids, you might say, in that big old house. From a hundred feet up, the roof with its two chimneys would have just blended in with thousands of others, jutting out from the thousands of trees standing sentinel over our storied town, best known for the witch trials held there in the late seventeenth century and a certain house with seven gables.

It was one of those houses that any kid would love to grow up in. There were so many rooms and stairwells and alcoves and they all provided endless opportunities for fort-building and hiding. I'll never forget those spots where I could hide forever—just me and my scraped knees surrounded by the look and feel of our house's beautiful old woodwork. When you walked in the front door, there was a formal staircase with a large banister that twisted up in a pattern of squared turns all the way to the top. I could stand on the first floor and look all the way up. At the back end of the house was another stairway, originally a service stairway, which rose from the kitchen to the top floor. That one was enclosed. With sixteen rooms, three bedrooms, a basement, and two stairwells, hide-and-seek was elevated to a varsity level.

Almost all my family members were musically inclined, and most of them played several instruments. While I always loved music, and while the memories of Dave Brubeck through the whole house on Saturday mornings are very dear to me, I just didn't get the musical gene. In a house full of musicians, I was the only one who didn't play an instrument or sing harmony. However, as early as the age of six or seven, I was obsessed with the idea of being a pilot. Logan Airport was due south of us, and I looked up into the sky over my neighborhood and watched countless planes going in and out of Boston.

I remember one airline that painted their planes bright yellow, and I loved to watch the big metal birds leave their contrails across the sky, imagining I was their pilot. At the time, the airline industry was growing and the wide-bodied jet was coming into fruition. McDonnell Douglas had their big DC-10, Boeing had the 747 jet, and Lockheed Martin had the L-1011. Just the sheer power and size of those aircraft fascinated me. Even though this was near the end of the Vietnam War, I wasn't really interested in high-performance aircraft yet. I was enamored with the whole commercial-airline industry and loved those big wide-bodied jets. By this time I had my own room overlooking the backyard and the walls were plastered with pictures of my heroes—pilots like Chuck Yeager and Amelia Earhart, and astronauts like Neil Armstrong and Buzz Aldrin.

Eventually, it wasn't enough to see the planes way up in the sky or on TV or even in my imagination. I wanted to get my hands on them. I would walk with my friends down to the local department store, Almy's, and check out the model airplanes made by a company called Revell. I started saving up my allowance and birthday money and even raking leaves or shoveling snow to earn money. I pretty much spent my money on model airplanes and movies. Some of the original models were pretty simple, but so much fun. I had a small mahogany school desk in my room, and I turned this into my work center. My dad gave me one of those gooseneck lamps, which stood in the corner of the desk.

If you ever made model airplanes or cars, you'll probably remember the excitement of opening the box. They always had cool photos on the lid and they always had that new-car smell when you started taking the parts out. I liked to open each box carefully and set it on its side near the edge of the desk so I always had a picture of what the plane should look like when I was done. The parts were shrink-wrapped, and I did my own inventory as I spread the parts out and read the instructions. Some of the smaller ones were mostly just an exercise in snapping parts together. They only took about ten or fifteen minutes to assemble, but I enjoyed the small parts, the precision required, and the smell of the paint.

My buddy Brad was a model-car freak and had quite a collection. Sometimes I packed up my collection in a box and transported it to Brad's house, where we would compare our craftsmanship. He showed me his model Mustangs or Barracudas, and the overall quality and precision always looked so much better than my airplanes. He knew how to use matches to create the look of exhaust and road grime on the tire wells, and he taught me that using spray paint was the way to go, especially on the larger parts.

I went through the first dozen models pretty fast and also made a lot of those simple balsa-wood glider planes. Whether it was gluing pennies to the nose to add stability or creating my own unique little rotors on the tail wings, I tried every imaginable experiment. I launched many wooden planes out my window, harassing the chickens that my dad always had in the backyard. After a while, there were a 747 and a couple of biplanes hanging at various angles from my ceiling. It was my own private aerodrome. I could soar, in my imagination, to my heart's content. While the rest of my family slept, I flew over the United States, across the Atlantic, all the way over Europe and Asia, crossing the Pacific and landing back in Salem. Here's the thing, though: I never built a helicopter. . . .

I built and built and graduated into more-complex models. I remember one day buying a DC-10 replica. I had saved some money, and I walked to Almy's department store and bought the plane. It felt like ten miles but it was probably only a few blocks. When I got home, I ran straight up to my room and got started. I opened the box and started pulling out all the parts. It was an American Airlines jet.

Over the next couple of weeks, the project became a competing priority with everything, even my homework. On the weekends, when my brothers and sisters were running around, I was in my room with my model airplane. I was late for dinner a few times, and in my household that was a capital crime. After assembling and painting every little detail, even the seats in the passenger area, I put the finishing touches on the exterior paint job with a can of spray paint in the backyard. As soon as it was dry, I carried it back up to my room and set it on my desk on its landing gear. I stood back and surveyed my work. It looked beautiful. It was kind of like the moment when Ralphie, in the movie *A Christmas Story,* finally got his Red Rider BB gun. I considered my building of that beautiful DC-10 model one of the greatest accomplishments of my life. Even then, as I looked at the completed model, I was thinking about the day when I'd get to sit in the cockpit and fly a plane just like that.

My First Time in the Sky

Probably every boy dreams of flying at one point, but very few ever have the chance to do it. One spring morning when I was twelve, I was sitting at the breakfast table with the whole family before school. It was a Monday, and as a kid that was not my favorite morning—an interruption to my weekend daydreams.

While everyone rushed to shovel food into their mouths and get out the door, my mother, a woman with blue eyes and auburn hair, smirked knowingly into her cereal for a few minutes before announcing, "Well, I won something in the church drawing yesterday, and I've decided to give it to Ray."

I stopped spooning my Lucky Charms and looked up at her. "You did?"

Smiling, she said, "Yes, and guess what?"

"What?"

"It's a free flying lesson in a real airplane!"

In the next instant I was jumping up and down, my arms wrapped around her, saying "thank you, thank you" over and over. I caught some jealous looks from my siblings at first, but I think they all understood how much flying would mean to me, and they never said a thing. It was excruciating going to school that day—all I could think about was flying.

I kept bugging my mom for every little detail about the plane all week. When Saturday finally rolled around, the whole family came along on the drive out to the Beverly, Massachusetts, Municipal Airport, which was more like an airstrip for small planes. We met the pilot instructor, a tall guy who was probably in his late twenties. He towered over me, with dark hair like mine and a serious expression that would break from time to time into a smile. Since he was the first real pilot I had ever met in person, I quickly added him to my growing list of personal heroes.

While my parents filled out some paperwork, I kept looking out the airport office windows at the little white Piper Cherokee with red stripes I'd soon be flying in. It was a tiny, single-engine plane with just enough room for a pilot, a copilot, and a little bit of cargo in the back, yet it dwarfed the model planes that covered the shelves in my room, and to me, that made it larger than life.

The pilot brought me into a small classroom in the back of the main terminal to discuss some of the safety precautions and other requirements. I wasn't expecting this part. I just wanted to fly. I couldn't stop looking around at the posters with safety messages and illustrations of aviation instruments and planes.

I was trying to pay attention, and nodding along with whatever he was saying, when suddenly he got very serious, bent down, and said, "If I tell you we have an emergency, I want you to do nothing but sit on your hands. If I have already issued you the controls, I will take them back from you. I need you to say nothing and sit on your hands." He wasn't joking.

I had never flown in a plane before, so when we walked out to the runway, it was the closest I had ever come to a real aircraft. He escorted me around the plane, which was only about twenty to twenty-five feet, and when we finally sat down in the cockpit, our shoulders were touching. I was speechless before the shiny, intricate detail of the instruments. My entire field of view was dominated by this huge instrument panel, and I could hardly see over it. These levers and dials and pedals and switches were all new to me. I wanted to click, push, pull, and press everything.

I was trying to act grown-up as the instructor gave me a brief orientation to the main controls. I kept nodding to indicate that I was paying attention, but I just wanted to fly! Then he started the engines and began to taxi toward the runway. We moved slowly. The sound of the engine roared in my ears. I kept one eye on the scene ahead of me, the runway rolling quickly below us, and the other eye on the pilot's hands. He began to pick up speed. He got faster and faster and, all at once, he lifted us off the ground! I felt that lift in my stomach. I was in the sky! I couldn't believe it. After building all those models and dreaming of being a pilot soaring over the earth, I was in the sky!

There was a set of tandem controls, typical in general-aviation airplanes. Once we were airborne, he let me handle the controls for a while and I could feel the plane respond when I pushed forward or pulled back or otherwise manipulated the controls, causing the plane to climb, dive, or roll. I could feel how sensitive the controls were to my touch. The pilot gave me some pointers, and I think I was a fast learner, but my strongest memory of that day was the view. For the next hour, we flew over our little town.

He pointed out certain landmarks and neighborhoods I barely recognized, and then we flew over my house, my school, and my friends' houses. From that altitude, my town looked like one of those towns you see under a Christmas tree with a toy train circling it. Even the Beverly Airport looked tiny from that elevation. At takeoff, the airport runway looked enormous. It was the biggest runway I'd ever seen. From that altitude, it was just a gray strip of asphalt carved into a field of green.

After maybe half an hour, the pilot took back the controls, and I sat wide-eyed as we drew closer to the runway. We got lower and lower. I was a little afraid, but I knew the pilot was in control. My family, below, slowly got larger, pointing up and clapping for me, my little brother Tommy jumping up and down. I felt like a hero. The pilot landed gently. I noticed the way he put the brakes on and stopped the plane exactly where he wanted. His control was incredible. After that day there was no doubt what I wanted to do with my life; I was hooked on flying. I wanted to be a pilot, just like that guy.

That was one day I'll never forget. As I got older, making model airplanes gradually was replaced, as it is with a lot of boys, by thinking a lot about girls. What can I say? It happens. I was starting to date and hanging out more with my friends, but one thing never changed: my dream of becoming a pilot. It only became stronger and stayed with me no matter what girl I met or friend I made. That day at the Beverly Municipal Airport gave me my goal in life.

A College with Wings

Life rolled on and I grew up, pretty much like any other guy. Between my sophomore and junior years of high school, my family moved to New Hampshire. I always had a job and was working as a dishwasher at the time, and I was almost sixteen. Seeing a way to use my dishwashing skills to hang out with friends and meet girls, I had signed up to work as part of the kitchen staff at a girls' summer camp. I mean, how great was that? A job *and* girls! I went there right after school let out that year. When the camp was over, my family picked me up and we drove to the new house in New Hampshire. All my boxes had been stuffed into my new room. I went off to the camp from Salem, Massachusetts and came back to a new neighborhood, a new high school, and a new city in New Hampshire.

I got a job as a waiter in one of the local restaurants, started dating a bit more seriously, and moved toward my final year of high school. And I still had no doubt about what I wanted to be. My dad wanted me to go to Boston College, but I had other plans. Even though there were more-inexpensive colleges nearby, such as the University of New Hampshire, I had my eyes on a private school called Nathaniel Hawthorne, which had a flight program. The idea of joining the military didn't even cross my mind.

I had been drooling over the college brochure, which featured scenic photos of the campus in the fall, and the DC-3 aircraft that was the workhorse of their flight program. When the school started advertising an open house for prospective students, my parents really didn't want to go, so I persuaded a couple of my buddies to go with me. We drove up for the open house and received a quick tour of the campus, which was very green and appealing to me. Before long we made our way to the small airport that was actually part of the school. I loved to see the pilots' lounge, to smell the fuel out on the runway, to see the little hangars and maintenance sheds all over, and especially to see the old DC-3 aircraft painted in the school colors with the Hawthorne College logo emblazoned on both sides.

I couldn't have been more excited when it was time for the flight. I knew that the DC-3 was the one of the original transport planes and had been used pretty extensively in WW II (when it was called a C-47, or Sky Train). I was impatient to fly. We received a short safety briefing and then approached the aircraft. It was a "tail dragger," so the tail sat low and the cockpit high. When we boarded, the plane was angled back, so we had to walk up a slight incline to find our seats. I got to see the cockpit briefly, but this wasn't another flying lesson just yet. This was a joy ride, and my buddies and I sat in the back with other kids, some of whom had their parents with them.

It was about a thirty-minute ride over the campus, and over the mountains of southern New Hampshire. They were trying to give the parents the best possible ride because they were also trying to "sell" the school and its flight program.

As I walked off the plane and talked to the pilot some more, I thought, *This is where I want to be.* Before we left that day, I made sure I had a handful of school information that included the application. Picturing myself as a student in this aviation program brought my dream of becoming a pilot to life.

My application was accepted, and when I graduated from high school in 1979, I packed up my stuff and eagerly relocated to the college campus. I bought an old Ford Maverick from my buddy Darren for $150, and it didn't even have a heater. I didn't care, as long as the car could make the one-hour drive between college and home.

Moving into the dorms was exciting, and before long I landed a job as a waiter near the school. I could still see my girlfriend on the weekends. I knew (and my parents reminded me) that this was an expensive proposition. First of all, it was a private school with high tuition. But more important, the flight program came with additional expenses that I wasn't sure how I was going to afford. My parents and my grandmother agreed to help out as much as they could. I also worked as much as possible, applied for every grant I could find, and maxed out the available student loans. Somehow, I patched together enough money to get started. I was an Aeronautical Science major who was officially earning his pilot's license.

I was required to enroll in the same academic core curriculum as any other major, but I also had to take courses like aeronautical science, transportation economics, and meteorology. In my young mind, these were the kinds of things pilots had to know,. At one point, I spent literally my last penny to buy a pair of aviation sunglasses. I thought I was pretty cool, all things considered.

My classmates and I were also indoctrinated into the pilot program. I met the flight instructors and set up my curriculum. Although each student went through the same training, they didn't necessarily go through it at the same pace. This was partly because some people struggle to learn different aspects of flying more than others do. But mostly it was a financial issue. Getting into the cockpit and up in the air was obviously a key part of the program, and you could actually fly as much as you wanted (within reason). But here was the catch: you had to maintain at least five hundred dollars in your flight account, and this was used to cover the one-hundred-dollars-per-hour cost for fuel, maintenance, and instructional flying.

As a waiter I was making a little over a dollar an hour plus tips and my flight account got drained very quickly. I didn't always have the money to replenish it. It didn't take me long to realize that I was going to school mostly with people whose families could afford to fund their educations. I remember using one of the pay phones in the training area one day, and a kid next to me said into the phone, "Hey, Dad, I need you to deposit another four thousand dollars into my flight account, okay?" I couldn't help but eavesdrop, and when the kid said "thanks," I was astounded to realize that his dad must have said "sure." My parents would have done the same thing if they could, no doubt in my mind, but they just couldn't. So, although I was keeping up with the classwork and overall syllabus, my limited flight account was keeping me on the ground way too much, and slowing down the best part of the program—flying!

Eventually, the cost of my tuition, books, and flight-program expenses became too much, and left me with a crucial choice: opt into a cheaper degree and give up the dream of flying or find another way to pay for college. I had six brothers and sisters, and I didn't want to place any additional burden on my parents, who had always been so supportive. I dropped out of the flight program and changed my major to Aviation Management. I wasn't depressed about it. I maintained a positive outlook, but I was disappointed with the realization that I wasn't going to be able to finish college, and take the necessary steps to finish pilot training all at the same time.

I needed a new plan.

CHAPTER 2

FROM BRAVO COMPANY TO HMX-1

Boot Camp, USMC Reserves, and College

Even though I grew up daydreaming about being a pilot, I really didn't know much about all those heroic pilots dropping Marines into combat zones under enemy fire. They were fighting overseas, defending us, and for me it was a world away. It was the Vietnam War era, a tough time for the military. Many people were unfortunately turning away from the armed forces.

Shortly after I dropped out of the flight program, something shifted. I had vaguely noticed Marine Corps recruiting pamphlets around campus, but I was already in flight school so I didn't pay them much attention. In fact, I had probably walked countless times past the small table in the cafeteria where the Marine recruiter hung out. Suddenly I was much more cognizant of the recruiting pamphlets, especially the ones about Marine Aviation. I noticed that some of the pamphlets were all about becoming a Marine pilot. There was also a video presentation on a continuous loop showing the various Marine aircraft. The videos were kind of corny and predictable, but I still liked them. Jets making sharp turns and leaving contrails across the sky. The afterburners lighting up as the aircraft took off into a fiery sunset. I think there might even have been a couple of helicopters in the video.

One day, instead of entering the cafeteria and just walking past the table, I stopped by. The Marine sitting there stood up, looked me right in the eye, and put his hand out. I shook his hand, and he introduced himself and asked my name. From that moment forward he called me by my first name.

"Are you in the flight program, Ray?"

"Well, I was, but I had to drop out because I couldn't afford the expenses." He caught me off guard, and I said too much too soon. I think I saw a little glimmer in his eye, and I think he knew he had me.

He immediately launched into an explanation of the Marine Corps aviation history, and told me that by joining the Marines I would have a chance to become a Marine pilot. The Marines would train me and pay for everything. I knew the rumors about recruiters, and while he was a nice guy who answered all my questions, I also knew that he was probably trying to meet a quota. Still, I had to admit that his uniform looked pretty sharp, and he seemed to have his stuff together.

I didn't want to rush into anything, but before I knew it I was filling out forms, we were playing phone tag, and then I took the initial evaluations to see if I met the basic requirements. The process had begun, and then it seemed almost inevitable. I also learned that you had to be an officer to become a pilot, and at that point I was only halfway toward my degree. The recruiter convinced me that it would be a good idea just to enlist as an infantryman first, to set the foundation for my career, and then I could decide about becoming an officer in a couple of years.

So that's exactly what I did. I became the first person in my family to join the military, and spent the next couple of years serving as an infantryman in the Marine Corps Reserves. But first, between my freshman and sophomore year of college, I had to go to boot camp at Parris Island, South Carolina.

In the Marine Corps, boot camp lasts twelve weeks—pretty much the entire summer break. To a certain degree, boot camp is like a factory that takes young men and women from all walks of life and transforms them into Marines. The training is broken up into three phases. There is a great deal of classroom instruction, but it's mostly hands-on training in the field. Marching and learning all the accurate drills is a major element of the disciplined environment, and you learn everything from marksmanship, to hand-to-hand combat, to tactical infantry maneuvers over and over again. The concepts of "team," "esprit de corps," and "brotherhood" are reinforced. I'm sure that to some degree, every Marine has similar experiences in boot camp. But we all end up seeing it differently depending on our state of mind, our physical abilities, and all those personal challenges we carry with us.

On the rainy day I headed off to boot camp in 1980, there was no fanfare, just me telling my wife and family goodbye at the Manchester Municipal Airport in New Hampshire. I could tell that my parents were proud, though Mom was anxious. I think they were nervous because they knew less about the Marine Corps than I did—and that wasn't much. I found myself sitting on plastic airport chairs with two other kids from the area. We swapped stories and proved just how little we knew. This was a completely new adventure for me. I had never even flown in a commercial aircraft.

As I boarded and found my seat, I admired the sheer size of this big Conair twin-engine plane. I did a quick mental assessment, comparing the gigantic airplane to the scale of my model airplanes. I surmised that the aircraft had probably been built in the fifties or sixties. The first leg of the flight was to LaGuardia International Airport in New York, and I had a seat just aft of the wing, giving me a clear view of all the aircraft's control movements. I took in every moment of the takeoff and landing and listened to the landing gear retract into the belly like talons under the body of a bird. When we touched down, we bounded and then touched down again, and I heard and felt the brakes. We switched planes and then flew into Savannah, Georgia. And that's where I got my first reality check.

I yawned and walked out of the terminal, stopping to hit the bathroom like any other traveler. I was still oblivious, just walking with my fellow recruits, wearing jeans and absorbing my surroundings. I had never even been away from home. And then we turned a corner and I saw a gaggle of other kids that looked just like me, anxious and unaware. It was a very diverse crowd, and as I walked up, a Marine approached and asked my name. I told him, then handed over the official orders my recruiter had told me to carry. The Marine checked me off a list with his pencil and directed me where to sit. I quickly realized that they were marshaling recruits from all over the country to move us to Parris Island together.

And then, right there in the middle of that crowd, something started happening. From somewhere, a domineering energy started to assert itself over the group. Loud, even angry voices were being raised and I thought, *What is going on here?* And, for the first time, I saw the famous Marine drill instructors. These were men who looked hardened; they were physically fit and steely-eyed and wore big wide-brim hats and perfectly starched uniforms. And they were not being kind. They seemed genuinely pissed that we were using up good oxygen. They were staring people down, intimidating us, playing the power game to see how we would react. My first thought was, *Jeez, we're civilians. We're in a public place. They can't treat us like that.* Boy, was I wrong. . . .

They were yelling at people to stay seated, and directing them exactly where to sit. Hundreds of us sat Indian-style in rows. As I looked around and nodded at the kids near me, and as I instinctively kept my head down and just kept quiet until I understood what was expected of me, I realized that I was now in the system. I still had on my jeans and sneakers, but I was definitely being treated like a recruit.

After a few hours it was time to load the buses. So far, I had been yelled at only a little, and I hadn't done anything except look around. That was all about to change. A dozen drill sergeants moved us through the crowd like ushers from Hell, herding and jostling us into the bus. "Get up and get on my bus." The ride from Savannah to Parris Island, in Beaufort, South Carolina, took about an hour, and there were about fifty kids on my bus. The bus was quiet and tense. You could have cut the tension with a knife, it was so thick. There were also a couple of drill instructors sitting up in the front row. Even they were being quiet, but I guessed correctly that it wouldn't last.

Everyone's eyes and ears perked up when we stopped at a guard gate briefly before driving into Parris Island. Everyone sat up straight. I remember looking down as we passed and seeing Marines standing guard who looked young like me. *That's my future,* I thought. Even though it was dark, I could see the old World War II–style building I had seen in movies, the linear landscaping and architecture that symbolize military bases. I saw the perfectly manicured training fields, and the trees everywhere, and I knew I had entered a whole new world.

When you first get off the bus at Parris Island, before you're even assigned to the company that you'll train with, you are inducted into the Marine Corps through a receiving barracks. This is the initial place they take you for basic medical evaluations, to assign you gear and uniforms, and to have you fill out tons of paperwork. When we pulled up to the receiving barracks, we were all looking out the bus windows, and I was getting a little nervous. You know that feeling you get that something very bad is about to happen? Well, that's the feeling I had. The bus rolled to a slow stop. The drill sergeants in the front of the bus stood up, turned around, and began screaming. More drill sergeants boarded the bus, and then all joined together in an angry chorus of demands and insults: "Are you stupid?"; "Can you hear me?"; "Do you know your right foot from your left?"; "Do you think this is a joke?"; "Do you want your mommy?"

There were hundreds of yellow footprints painted in formation right there on the street. They looked like the soles of two boots spread a few inches apart and facing outward at a forty-five-degree angle. The drill instructors were pissed off and impatient. They wanted us to keep our bags off the ground and move in an orderly manner. It felt more like complete chaos, and I quickly realized that even if you do exactly what you're told, it's still wrong. Nobody was going to be right. None of us knew a damn thing. We were screwed up and they took every opportunity to point out just how much.

I stood on the yellow footprints and tried to stare straight ahead as they were yelling at us to do. But this caused a dilemma because many of the drill instructors were also yelling at people, "Don't look at me. Look straight ahead." This didn't work when they stood right in front of you and stared in your face. All I could hear after a while were the various drill instructors yelling over one another, because us recruits were saying very little except "sir, yes sir," or whatever they told us to say.

I had been told what to do by teachers and parents and bosses lots of times. I could take direction. But it was never this kind of aggressive, demeaning, apparently blind fury. I knew (or hoped I did) that they wouldn't hurt me physically, so I just did exactly what I was told. I tried to blend in, but sometimes I looked up and made eye contact, and got yelled at. It was almost like I'd just gotten caught in the line of some drill instructor's fire. Just hours earlier, I had been back in New Hampshire. A college kid. Now, I was a Marine recruit standing at attention in a place I didn't know, being yelled at by drill instructors who could snap me in two, if they wanted to. I was scared shitless.

Eventually, we were broken down into groups and assigned to a squad bay in the receiving barracks. In what would become three months of learning a new culture and vocabulary, I soon learned that a bed was a "rack." When we began the process of filling out paperwork, everyone had to sit down and write a short letter home. It was a form letter, and basically said, "Hi, Mom and Dad. I've arrived. I'm okay. Don't call me. I'll call you." Within a day, my head was shaved and I looked like everyone else. Individuality was discouraged. All my civilian belongings had been taken until after graduation, and I was issued a sea-bag that contained my new wardrobe—camouflage utility uniforms and PT clothes.

Next, they assigned me to Delta Company, Platoon 2028, 2nd Recruit Training Battalion. When I went to sleep in my strange and jarring new environment, surrounded by unknowns, the shady breezeways and cozy library of Nathaniel Hawthorne College seemed very far away.

To put it simply, boot camp is designed to break you down, mentally and physically, and then use that clean slate to build you back up as a Marine. I did pretty well with the mental part of boot camp. Inside, it took some getting used to. Part of you wants to scream back and then another part doesn't dare to blink an eye. With so many people and personalities, there were lots of different reactions. Some kids seemed to have it together and just took it in stride. Other kids, even some who thought they were tough, just wilted under the gaze of the drill instructors, and broke down in tears.

Whether we were drilling for hours on end until everyone's heels clicked at the same exact time, or whether we were being forced on a twelve-mile hump with packs on sandy and treacherous trails, I just gritted my teeth and pushed on. One night in the first week, I was one of a row of those kids we've all seen in movies standing at attention at the foot of their racks at 3:00 A.M. while the drill instructors screamed because the floor wasn't shiny enough. My name wasn't so easy to spell or pronounce, and I actually think it saved me from being called out so much in the beginning.

Nevertheless, the drill instructors were masters at the art of sensing and exploiting any weakness, any individuality. I mostly stayed out of trouble, and out of the way, and learned to compartmentalize my feelings when a grown man was standing with his nose inches from mine, breathing his lunch in my face, and screaming at me as if I had personally offended his mother. As I was forced to do countless push-ups, sit-ups, leg squats, or other exercises until I reached muscle failure, I don't remember ever crying. But I do remember being angry, being scared, wanting to rebel, and feeling frustrated as I was constantly punished and corrected, even for someone else's mistake. More than once, I thought to myself, *Holy shit. Did I make a big mistake? These guys are nuts. What in the hell am I doing here?*

As I got better at controlling my emotions and showing only a blank mask of obedience to the drill instructors, I was able to see through the immediate intensity and focus on the larger lessons I was being taught: Follow orders. Pay attention to details. Don't try to be an individual. Do what's best for the overall organization. Look out for your brothers in arms. Another thing that was ingrained in us from day one was diversity and acceptance. It didn't matter where someone was from or what they looked like. The drill instructors made it crystal clear that there were only two kinds of Marines: light green Marines and dark green Marines. Period.

The Vietnam War had just ended and most of the drill instructors had Vietnam campaign ribbons on their uniforms. These were battle-hardened Marines, fresh from the conflict in Southeast Asia, and now they were focusing every ounce of their energy and attention on making sure we could follow in their footsteps. Or else. They had been trained to instill in us the Marine ethos, a mental and physical toughness that would drive us to overcome any obstacle put in our way.

Everyone knew that they really weren't supposed to hit us, but the drill instructors were covering for one another. They certainly wouldn't hesitate to slap or punch someone in the gut. At one point in the training we learned close combat with "Pugil sticks." Imagine long sticks with fairly hard pads on each end, like a giant Q-tip. We had to stand in the center of the group and face off against one another, or compete against other squads and platoons. My platoon actually won the Pugil stick competition, and one of the drill instructors started carrying a Pugil stick around with him everywhere. Many times while we were standing in formation being yelled at for something, this particular drill sergeant would walk down the line looking for any reason to instill discipline. When he was displeased with something about how you looked or sounded, he would just pop you in the head with the end of the Pugil stick. I watched him do this a few times through my peripheral vision, and felt lucky when he passed me without hitting me in the face.

As a kid and in high school, I had never been more than generally interested in sports or exercise. I certainly played sports as a kid, and I was pretty good when I applied myself. During high school I was more busy partying with my friends and dating than worrying about any kind of fitness. Likewise, I didn't pursue any sports in college. Sure, I hit the gym a little bit here and there, but it wasn't a big focus of my life at all. I would say I was in average shape when I arrived at boot camp. Very early on, we had to do an inventory physical fitness test, or PFT. The test consisted of pull-ups, a three-mile run, and sit-ups. Of course, everyone was comparing their performance and competing. A lot of people couldn't pass even the most basic physical requirements, while some kids scored the maximum of 300 on their first physical fitness test. I fell somewhere in the middle.

During this period I was eating like a madman, drinking huge volumes of water, absorbing so much training, sweating off body fat I didn't know I had, and running more than I ever thought possible. I was getting whipped into the best shape of my life in a relatively short period of time, and I noticed. I was getting faster on each run, and I liked it. Over the course of boot camp, I progressed physically from somewhere in the middle to much closer to the high end. Boot camp is truly where my lifelong love of fitness and running took root, and led me to compete in many triathlons later in life.

By design, most people go through an internal shift at around week nine or ten. By that point, you have been there long enough that you are immersed, mentally and physically. You like the way you feel, the growing strength and energy, and you take pride in reducing the frequency with which you screw up. It definitely happened to me. In that little microcosm of 2nd Battalion on Parris Island in 1980, I did take pride when my platoon did the right thing. It felt good when we looked sharp and made our turns and stops in unison. It felt so good to triumph over the other groups in competition. It felt good to run faster and harder and longer. I was becoming a Marine.

During the first few weeks, I noticed groups that had arrived before us. They looked different because they had been working hard, and it showed. They also looked different because they were allowed to "blouse" their trousers. This meant that instead of their trousers just hanging loosely near the bottoms of their boots, which made them look generally sloppy, they put these little blousing bands inside the bottoms of their trousers. Now their trousers seemed to stop around the top of the boot. This was how Marines should look, and we did not.

As we neared the final month of boot camp, we were told to carry our blousing bands in our pockets. We weren't deserving enough to use them yet, of course, but we at least could hope. After dragging it out over and over and really building it up, we finally performed one single task very well. The drill instructor was pleased. Finally, he gave us the order to "blouse boots!" From that point on, we were the cool guys. We were the ones that the new recruits looked up to.

The biggest physical and mental challenge of the entire three months, again by design, was a simulated war exercise that took place at Elliot Beach (we called it "EB"). It was like a big final exam in which you were pushed and tested in everything you had learned mentally, physically, and tactically. It was a big deal, and failing in that exercise could easily get you sent home. It wasn't supposed to test just our personal mettle; this was about coming together as a team. I made it through, and I learned even more about myself and the power of teamwork. We completed that exercise and marched back to the barracks, and we knew that the rest of our time was going to be smooth sailing—admin, paperwork, and getting ready for graduation. I stood with a deep sense of accomplishment and pride at the Emblem Ceremony, where we were all presented with the infamous Eagle, Globe and Anchor emblem that personifies the Marine Corps.

I was in the best shape of my life, I felt like after that I could handle just about anything, and I definitely shared that perverse pride that comes with completing boot camp. I had never been so proud of anything as that moment at graduation when they addressed us as Marines for the first time in twelve long weeks. About seventy-five of us had started, and about fifty-five of us had earned the title of United States Marine.

When I returned to New Hampshire to continue my college studies, I was still Ray L'Heureux, but—even though I thought I hadn't—I had changed: I felt stronger and more confident in almost every aspect of my life, and I enjoyed being a new Marine. I was assigned to Bravo Company, 25th Marines, a Marine Reserve detachment in Manchester, New Hampshire. I trained with them one weekend a month while I finished my degree. I also began seriously to think about the idea of becoming an officer and a Marine pilot. Along with all the other big steps I was taking at the time, I took one more: I got married. And then it happened: during my junior year of college, Dianna and I had our first child, Ray Jr., in July 1982. Besides being a new Marine, I was now also a proud dad and I said to myself, "Go for it!"

That's all it took. I began to coordinate with the Officer's Selection office in Manchester. Eventually, I secured a guaranteed aviation spot, which meant a new set of contracts. I would no longer be a Marine Reservist. Now I was going to be an officer candidate who would enter active duty after graduating from college. If I made it through OCS and all the flight training, I would "owe" the Marine Corps six years of service in exchange for my training.

Officer Candidate School and Early Flight Training

I graduated from Nathaniel Hawthorne College in May 1983, with a Bachelor's Degree in Aviation Management. My daughter Delia was born that day, and then I shipped back out to Marine Base Quantico. It was time for OCS, which included ten weeks of officer training completely focused on developing Marine officers. At boot camp, the PT went from easier to more difficult. At OCS, we did PT all the time. It was intense and some of the grueling obstacle courses defined the word *grueling*.

We also spent a lot of time in the classroom. We learned foundational leadership skills, core principles, tactics, and Marine Corps history we would need to someday lead Marines. Most important, we were placed in varying leadership roles in the platoon and rigorously evaluated and coached on our performance. Again, poor performance could get you sent home.

Ten weeks passed, and I graduated near the top of my class at OCS. I was a 2nd Lieutenant—a Marine officer—and I left Quantico even more determined to become a Marine aviator. Just a couple of months later, I was right back at Quantico for The Basic School. This course was required for all new Marine officers and was my last obstacle before starting flight school! In my mind, The Basic School was a natural extension of OCS, and it further developed the skills I would need to lead and mentor Marines.

In the spring of 1984, I moved to Pensacola, Florida, the cradle of Marine Corps aviation, and finally entered the Aviation Indoctrination Program at the Naval Air Station there. This is where all Navy, Marine Corps, Coast Guard, and even some international pilots begin their flight training. We initially rented a home just a few miles from base and lived there for the next two years.

I started the training with around twenty other people, but it's a very dynamic, challenging, and competitive process. Approximately 50 percent of the class didn't graduate. And there were plenty of ways to wash out of the training: you could have been psychologically unfit to fly or unable to handle the physical demands. People are held back or kicked out for poor performance, medical issues, or any number of other reasons. So, you get ahead of some of your buddies, or get behind them, but you pretty much see many of the same faces throughout your two years there. Additionally, there are always classes that started ahead of you and new classes beginning. I was just one of maybe a thousand faces somewhere inside that big, complex training cycle.

Here's the real killer: everyone knew that if you didn't graduate from flight school, you got "grounded" but still had to finish your active-duty commitment. I knew there was nothing wrong with being part of the ground forces, but that wasn't my goal. Compared to college, boot camp, OCS, and The Basic School, for me this was the most exciting. I probably never wanted anything so badly. My attitude was that I had made the choice to be there, I had taken on the commitment, so I might as well pour my heart and soul into the training.

The training was set up in a "crawl-walk-run" style of syllabus that is very common in the military. This meant I learned one small step at a time, but each new step built on the last. We started with six weeks in a classroom before even touching an aircraft, including courses like Basic Engineering, Meteorology, and Aerodynamics. I was so excited that the information learned in the classroom could be parlayed into the cockpit, and I was intent on being a great student. The thought of flying kept me on the books.

Being a Marine meant working with a dynamic and ever-changing cast of characters that inspired me, taught me, and made me laugh, while a few of them become lifelong friends. I forged a relationship with Steve Paquette during this period. He is one of those people. Steve is from Chippewa Falls, Wisconsin. He's the kind of person everyone wants to be around, and he has an infectious laugh.

Steve and I, and other buddies we met along the way, would study together and test each other's knowledge. Once we completed the rigorous academic portion of the training, we moved to nearby Whiting Field, Florida, to begin the actual flight training. Since I was married, I lived in base housing with my wife and two young kids. First up, I was introduced to the T-34 Charlie, a turbo-charged aircraft that the Navy used as a basic flight-training plane. It's about the same size as the Piper Cherokee I had taken my first lesson in as a kid, but the T-34 could fly circles around that little commercial aircraft. It was a two-seater with a jet engine, so it was "acrobatic." Part of the training included doing loops, rolls, half loops, split S's, and a slew of other stunts. I thought, *All right, this is way cooler than the Piper Cherokee I started learning to fly back in college!*

I started spending more and more time in the air around the Florida coast, learning to fly and maneuver as they led us through yet another crawl-walk-run syllabus. I was also learning all the safety and emergency procedures. Water-survival training was one of the more intense parts of this phase. The first step was to go through "drown proofing," which included several mental and physical tests, like swimming a mile and treading water with twenty-five pounds of full flight gear on, including my Nomex flight suit, steel-toed boots, gloves, a survival vest, and a heavy helmet.

The biggest challenge that everyone talked about was "The Dunker." Imagine a mock cockpit with no doors, and then imagine being seated in that pretend cockpit with all your seatbelts and safety straps secured and buckled tightly, and then being blindfolded. Now imagine that cockpit dropping into and sinking to the bottom of an Olympic-size swimming pool. The Dunker was one of the most feared courses in the school, designed to simulate crashing in water and escaping a sinking aircraft. Before any Marine could fly, he had to dunk.

On the day of the test, some people pretended to be very excited. Others were obviously scared to death. I had already watched a couple of classmates freak out under the water, so when it was my turn, I tried my best to keep my cool. I had paid attention in the briefing and I knew that the key was to stay calm and follow procedures. I climbed in and an instructor secured all my safety belts and then blindfolded me. He explained that my goal was to "release your safety harness, climb out of the cockpit, and swim to the surface." I nodded, taking lots of deep breaths while I still could.

And then it was time. After a short countdown, the cockpit slid backward and crashed through the surface of the water, flipping end-over-end as it sank to the bottom. I was completely disoriented as the cockpit filled with water, the stinging scent of chlorine filling my nose. I managed to gulp a large breath of air just before the little cabin filled up completely. I felt lucky. Some of my classmates hadn't gotten that breath in time, and it cost them.

Following the training precisely, I unstrapped myself and, using my right hand, located the right side of the cockpit. I tripped the release lever and worked my way out and into the open water. Remembering a trick my instructor had taught me, I blew bubbles to get my bearings, trying to remain calm and not give in to the instinct to start swimming frantically until I knew which way was up. Agonizing seconds went by as I let a few precious air bubbles escape and waited for them to slide across my face, in whichever direction the surface was. Finally I got my bearings, and burst to the surface as fast as I could. I heard my classmates cheering when my head appeared above the water. I had passed The Dunker, but I hoped never to have to use those skills in real life.

It was exhilarating to fly the T-34 and learn all the various aspects of being a Marine pilot, but halfway through the program, we all had to start the process of "selecting" which type of aircraft we wanted to fly: helicopters or jets. I wasn't very clear or even concerned at that point about which type of aircraft I would be trained to fly. I was just happy to be there at all.

I knew that if I got selected for jets, I would have to move to Texas, or one of the Navy's other jet-training bases, since there was no jet training in Pensacola. At the time, the F-18, the sleek Marine fighter seen in movies like *Independence Day* and *Behind Enemy Lines,* was a brand-new aircraft, and most of my buddies wanted to fly those. For some reason, I really had no desire to fly jets. Maybe because they weren't the huge birds floating across the sky of my boyhood memories back in Salem. And although I had never been in a helicopter, I was intrigued by the precision required to control rotary-wing aircraft.

Similarly, we had to decide on which bases we would like to be stationed. I could also arrange my selections based on "coast," so the choices were East, West, or Hawaii. Finally, I could place a stronger emphasis on location than aircraft. This was like saying, "If I get stationed in the place I choose, then I don't care what aircraft I fly, helicopter or jet. Duty location is more important to me than choice of aircraft." Finally, I could place the emphasis on a type of aircraft over location, and they would try to find you a position somewhere flying that particular aircraft.

This was yet another competitive selection process, based on your performance throughout the training. Steve and I turned in our top three choices, selecting either Hueys, Cobras, or CH-46s or CH-53s. At the young age of twenty-four I knew I wanted two things: to explore a different coast and to fly something very different from what I was accustomed to. I had never been to Hawaii, so I basically said, "I'll fly anything you throw at me as long as I get to live in Hawaii." In fact, at that point in my life I had never been west of the Mississippi. But I also knew that whatever my preference, my assignment would ultimately come down to the needs of the Marine Corps.

I was selected to fly helicopters, but nothing was guaranteed. As always, there was another hurdle to overcome. I still had to complete my helicopter training at the Navy Helicopter Training Squadron on the other side of Whiting Field. I received an entirely different set of gear, and then checked into Training Squadron HT-18. For the next six months, the same type of rigor applied, including extensive classroom instruction and then lots of time in the cockpit.

We started off with three weeks of ground school, attending classes on helicopter aerodynamics, engineering, FAA regulations, and safety procedures. Since we were already pilots, this was more-specialized training. The stakes seemed to be higher and the academic regimen even more intense. Class standing was directly related to selection and assignments, so failing a test could actually get you bounced from the course.

As we moved closer to getting in the air, we used a "static cockpit trainer" to become familiar with being inside a cockpit. In these stand-alone cockpits, I learned all the basic switchology and emergency procedures, in preparation for the real thing. Just as I had learned in the T-34, and just as every pilot in virtually every aircraft did, the cockpit procedures revolved around a series of detailed checklists. There are checklists covering pre-flight, start-up, engine shutdown, post-flight, and more. And each one has a series of "challenge-response" steps, in which one person reads off the commands and the other performs the correction action and replies with the appropriate response. In a typical flight, the pilot and copilot have this verbal exchange, but there in the training helicopter, the instructor was reading off the commands and watching my every move.

Not unlike the classroom-testing portion of the course, if you did not perform to standard, you received what we called a "down." Otherwise known as a failure. To get a "down" on two flights, or on two written tests for that matter, you had to stand before a board that would assess whether or not you had what it took to continue. Cockpit procedures are a major, integral part of flight training, and everyone knew it. I had posters on the wall of my office that showed all the switches, buttons, and gauges in the cockpit. I spent many hours studying those posters and memorizing every little word on the checklists.

But learning cockpit procedures in my room and applying them in the actual cockpit trainer with the instructor watching were two different things. When he called them out, it better be obvious that I knew what to do and what to say. I'd better not be "hunting" for switches, or I'd most definitely receive a "down." I had a flawless training record so far, and I wasn't about to mess that up.

"Fuel selector valve."

"Open."

"Auxiliary power unit."

"Start."

"Sequencing flashing lights."

"Flash."

The next step was the simulator, called the Cockpit Procedures Trainer (CPT). The simulator did not involve any motion, but it did help me to get even more familiar with the overall feel and functions of a helicopter cockpit.

Finally, it was time. We trained on the Bell Jet Ranger, which is a very common, small helicopter still in use today by many local TV news stations. Not unlike the static trainer, sitting in the cockpit felt like sitting in a bubble-shaped greenhouse. There were some major differences between this and the T-34 I had learned to fly prior to helicopter training. First of all, the T-34 was a small plane that sat on wheels. The Bell Jet Ranger was a small helicopter that sat on skids. The T-34 had a tandem cockpit, meaning that the instructor pilot was always in a seat right behind me. But in the Bell Jet Ranger, I sat right next to my instructor pilot.

After some additional training on start-up and shutdown procedures, safety, and troubleshooting, we began to cycle through our actual helicopter flight training broken up into a series of familiarization flights we called FAMs. When it was my turn for FAM, the instructor pilot and I climbed into the helicopter and he took the controls. I was serious and attentive, but inside I was thinking, *This is so incredibly cool. Let's get up in the air!*

The instructor started up the bird and began to do an "air taxi" from the parking area to the runway. As soon as he lifted the skids just a few feet off the ground, I experienced a very new feeling. This was nothing like picking up speed down the runway and then using momentum to take off. Instead, we were hovering right above the ground and still moving forward. I watched his hands and feet and tried to follow his movements in relation to the simulator training.

Once we made it to the runway and he called over the radio for the proper clearances, he began to lift directly up into the air and fly us over to the large grassy area where all the helicopter flight training took place. There were dozens of helicopter-landing pads below us, and he landed on one of them. The first time I performed all the start-up procedures in a real helicopter was intense. As the instructor called off the various commands from the checklist, the helicopter actually responded. I had to focus my mental energies and hand–eye coordination, because the smell of jet fuel, the sound and feel of the engines starting, and various lights coming on threatened to break my concentration.

One of the very first and most fundamental skills a helicopter pilot must learn is the art of hovering. Since a helicopter lifts straight off the ground, you take off and land by hovering, and it is a central part of flying helicopters in general. Hovering is a very difficult thing to teach and a very difficult thing to do, but I would learn out on those fields. There are three main functions. First, there is the "stick" right in front of you and between your legs. This is called the "cyclic," and it controls the angle of the rotor blades. Then there is the stick in your left hand, called the "collective," which controls the pitch of the rotor blades. By pulling on the collective, you lift the aircraft up into the sky. Finally, there are the rudder pedals, which turn the nose of the aircraft and change the angle of the tail rotor. I had to learn to perform all three of these functions at the same exact time, seamlessly. The cyclic is the hardest part to master, because there is a natural tendency to "control the stick." When this happens, you aren't hovering, you are just all over the place.

The instructor used several key techniques to teach me. First, he took us up to about 25 feet, turned the helicopter, and told me to "ride the controls" with him. This meant that he was flying the aircraft, but I could feel what he was doing. I then rode the controls as he landed and took off a few more times. Next, he had me work the pedals only, while he did everything else. He carefully "guarded the controls," in case I screwed up, and instructed me to turn the pedals while in midair to see how it felt. It was time for me to lift off. I was very unsteady, but I did it.

The hand–eye coordination required to hover was unlike anything I had experienced in a cockpit before. To a passenger, it could feel like the aircraft might succumb to gravity and drop out of the sky at any moment, like floating on an invisible cushion of air. But to the pilot, the act (and art) of hovering actually had physical sensations associated with it. With the pressure of the stick in my hand, the pedal under my foot, I could actually "feel the hover." In other words, the physics and mechanics of hovering actually gave me "feedback" through the controls, and it felt wonderful as I started to "get it."

One of the most popular T-shirts in the gift shop on base made light of the long-standing (and usually good-mannered) polarity between jet pilots and helicopter pilots. The shirt read, TO FLY IS HEAVEN . . . TO HOVER IS DIVINE. After learning how to do both, I couldn't have agreed with the joke more. Over the next week or so, during the FAM stage, I had gotten pretty good at lifting off and was hovering steadily on my own. That's when the real growth began, and each time I flew I got smoother and more confident.

We moved into the next level of training, which was called "pattern work." Part of the field had large, square patterns painted on the ground, and I had to "slide" the helicopter down each side of the square, following the lines precisely and making sharp turns at the ninety-degree angles. Over time, my instructor pilot integrated all the instrumentation, so that I was eventually flying totally on my own. And after a few months of that, I was learning to control the helicopter in more tactical movements, such as following the terrain and flying "near as possible" or NAP of the earth. I had already learned how to fly the T-34 and made successful solo flights. Now I had learned to start, take off, maneuver, hover, and land an entirely different kind of aircraft with new aerodynamic principles. This was a huge rite of passage and brought me one step closer to the fleet. I felt larger than life, and probably walked with just a bit more swagger. I know that a lot of my buddies shared the feeling.

I knew that part of the training involved a cross-country flight like

I had done in the T-34. I was excited when the time approached, because I knew I would get to work on my long-range navigational planning. On top of that, I had heard how fun it was to fly down to Key West and back, with some downtime in between. My partner in the cross-country flight was my buddy Ron Colyer. The instructor did the flying, and Ron and I did all the navigation.

It took us the better part of the day to get to Key West, as we had to traverse the entire Florida Panhandle and make a couple of fuel stops. We flew between 1,000 and 2,000 feet over the land, until we hit the Atlantic coast. At that point, we turned south and dropped our altitude to about 200 feet. I was amazed as we flew over Palm Beach, looking down at all the mansions, swimmers, surfers, and beachgoers. As far as I could see, there was powder-white sand to my right and aquamarine water to my left.

When we landed at Naval Air Station Key West, we buttoned up the aircraft and headed over to the officer's quarters. We each changed into civilian clothing, picked up a rental car, and headed out for some dinner and drinks. After idolizing the flight instructor for so long, it was a treat to be able to hang out with him. And since the only kind of unit I had ever been in was a training unit, this experience gave me a small taste of what it would be like to hang out with my fellow pilots after the work was done.

Three years after graduating from college, and after about eight months of intensive flight training, I became a fully instrument-rated solo pilot, with some pretty decent skills. I earned my Marine Corps aviator wings on May 16, 1986. I felt like a kid all over again on graduation day as I stood in formation and scanned the crowd for my family. My wife and kids were there, along with my father-in-law and sister-in-law. My brother Roger had even driven in to show his support.

My recruiter had been right about one thing: I didn't have to worry about keeping my "flight account" full anymore. I also didn't have to work after class to pay for the training. Now, the training had become my job, and I loved every minute of it. I had achieved and even exceeded my childhood dreams of becoming a pilot, and I was a Marine!

Now that I had earned my wings and the initial training was finally over, the clock officially began on my six-year active duty commitment. There were no slots available in Hawaii at the time, but both Steve and I got one of our wishes, and we were assigned to the same unit flying massive CH-53 helicopters in California. I relocated my family to California, totally energized about starting my very first assignment in the Marine Corps.

Air Station Tustin—My First Active Duty Assignment

My first active duty assignment was at Air Station Tustin, California. The original name of the base was Tustin, LTA, an old WW II "Lighter than Air" (LTA) base. There are actually still two blimp hangars standing from WW II, and they are some of the largest freestanding wooden structures in the country.

The CH-53 was a huge helicopter that could carry up to forty-two combat-equipped Marines, with six titanium rotor blades that weighed four hundred pounds each. This was a big and loud aircraft that you could hear coming from a long way off. Flying this war machine always entailed a mix of adrenaline, brute force, the strong smell of jet fuel, and the pure joy of handling two 4,000-horsepower jet engines. As expected, I had to go through even more training just to be able to fly the CH-53.

Once we were certified to fly, Steve and I were assigned to HMH-363, also known as the Red Lions, a moniker the unit earned during Vietnam. Since its inception, the Marine Corps helicopter community has designated its aircraft in a few ways, depending on the sizes and capabilities. Among others, there is the Helicopter, Marine Heavy

(HMH); the Helicopter, Medium Light (HML—also called Hueys); and the Helicopter, Marine Attack (HMA—also called Cobras). These classifications are also sometimes used to name organizations, such as HMH-363, the Red Lions, or HMX-1 (originally called Marine Helicopter Experimental Squadron One).

As anyone who has ever been in the military can tell you, there is a major difference between a training environment and your actual duty station. Even if you stay for only a year or so, and even if you have to go through six more months of advanced helicopter training right when you get there, you don't feel like a transient anymore.

I met Scott "Bayou" Minaldi and Craig "Spanky" Clement during my time in Tustin, and they both became lifelong friends as well. Bayou was a tall, dark ladies' man from Louisiana; a slick southern gentleman who was one of the best pilots I've ever met. Spanky was a blond-haired, blue-eyed Catholic from Virginia with a great sense of humor. He could fix anything you put in front of him, from engines to houses.

Growing up in New England, the beach had never been a big part of my experience. It was always too cold. But California was my new home, and I fell in love with it immediately. I really had the best of both worlds. Even in the line of duty, I was flying over the coast during training, enthralled by the seemingly endless horizon and the land jutting out into the water. On weekends we would get together and explore coves and beaches, trails and mountains on foot or on bike, and during the week we might fly a massive helicopter over the very same spots. I began to appreciate the fact that I got to see things in a way that many people never will. From boats to surfers, to the rooftops and trees in the area, I saw it all through the magical lens of the helicopter's cockpit.

It was also there at Tustin that I met two people who would become my greatest mentors and supporters throughout my career: my commanding officers, Lieutenant Colonel Richard "Willie" Willard and Lieutenant Colonel Ned Paulson. Steve and I never hit it off with the first CO, as he didn't pay us much attention. When Willie took over, he became the first CO who saw my potential and personally mentored me. He was known in the community as "Mr. 53" because he knew the CH-53 aircraft so well. He was technically brilliant and extremely serious about teaching us to fly in combat, but he also knew how to kick back in the Officer's Club. To put it simply, Willie was legendary in the community, and larger than life. He's probably the best 53 pilot I ever flew with. You couldn't help but respect his presence, his rank, his leadership, and his technical expertise, but more than that, he treated us as human beings. He created an environment based on high performance standards, but one in which you could also make and learn from mistakes.

Not only did I see something in Willie, he saw something in me. Shortly after I became an Aircraft Commander, he did one of my check rides. As I became a bit more seasoned, he assigned me as the Naval Air Training and Operating Procedures Standardization (NATOPS) Officer. This was an important role in virtually every Navy, Coast Guard, or Marine squadron. Not only that, but this was a position usually reserved for more-senior Captains, since the NATOPS Officer rode with the CO and performed check rides on other pilots. Nevertheless, Willie felt that I was the right person for the job. Willie mentored Steve as well, and Steve would sometimes tease me for being the teacher's pet, but I didn't mind.

Again, this didn't feel like training anymore, although we still participated in lots of training missions. Now I was a member of an organization that had a proud history, and that felt like an extension of my family. We went to countless barbecues and social events, and the kids were just getting old enough to start school. Like every married Marine, I tried to balance work with family. When Willie finally retired and we found out we were going to get a new Commander, we were all a bit disheartened. But as it turned out, we were so lucky to get Ned. He was Greek and had huge brown eyes that could look right through you. He also had a loud voice and a personality that could fill up a room with its intensity. He took me under his wing as well, and one of his greatest strengths was putting the right people in the right jobs. Once he put you in a position, he gave you his absolute trust to do your job, and the resources and support you needed to be successful.

Ned was always protective of his Marines. I once accompanied Ned to a high-level meeting with a full bird Colonel, and the Colonel was trying to micromanage what he wanted Ned to do. I think my mouth must have been open for a few seconds when Ned said, "With all due respect, sir, keep your fucking hands off my squadron." That's how seriously Ned took his job. I worked extremely hard to meet and exceed the Commander's guidance, and played just as hard when time allowed. This was the period in my life when I became really active in the local culture of endurance competitions, which involved a combination of swimming, running, and biking.

Between 1986 and 1988, I was promoted to Captain and went on three overseas deployments in Thailand, the Philippines and Japan, and Korea. I had already flown and traveled more than I ever would have imagined just a few short years earlier. There was no war going on at the time, but we still called this a deployment. Due to a national security agreement with Japan, virtually any Marine stationed in the Pacific was going to spend some time in Japan. At the time, we still had two large military bases in the area. On the first deployment, I had never been out of the country, so this was like going on an international field trip with my fraternity brothers—but with the ultimate toys!

While there, we flew in three major multinational training exercises. Although the CH-53 was a workhorse, it was also prone to maintenance issues back then. This knowledge made it very interesting to fly with nine or ten other CH-53s from Okinawa to the island of Luzon for training. Once we left Okinawa, we didn't see land again for eight hours. We had safety procedures for crash landings in the water, and I had never forgotten The Dunker training back in flight school, but none of us wanted to land in the water unless there was no other option. So there was a running joke during the trips that if a warning light started going off in the cockpit, just stick a piece of gum over it, because there was nothing you could do about it.

Luckily, we all made it in one piece, and then we stopped to refuel in a slick little operation called Rapid Group Refueling (RGR). We landed in a remote area on the island of Batan. Basically, a huge C-130 full of fuel lands in this remote area—the Marine Corps' traveling gas station. We would land nearby, hook up the hoses, and get fueled up again for the next leg. We took off and flew a while longer, until we hit the northern coast of Luzon. Then we followed the coast all the way to Subic Bay, north of Manila.

Steve and I shared a dorm-style room right across the street from the Officer's Club, which we frequented whenever we had some downtime. In those moments, after flying a CH-53 all day, and bellying up to the bar for a few drinks, we would smile with the knowledge that we were living the dream. We were copiloting these complex tactical aircraft in what felt like a very exotic setting, and even though we were separated from our families, we were also having fun.

We also made the kinds of memories that probably seemed funny only to us. One Friday night, I was sound asleep after an evening of drinking and socializing and a long week at work. Steve stumbled into the room at three in the morning. I squinted up at him, and he said, "Holy crap, my wife just went to the hospital. I'm going down to get a flight home right now."

This was some big news he had obviously been expecting, but the reality of it seemed to have him stunned. For some reason, the smallest detail has always stuck with me. We had just gone to the commissary and stocked up on food few days earlier, and just before Steve walked out of the room to fly across the ocean to meet his new baby, he seemed to recall this important fact.

He turned back and said, "Frenchy, eat my food," and then left.

When I returned from that first deployment a few months later, I felt pretty salty, pretty accomplished. I was an international traveler, after all! At a certain point, I had the option to leave the Marine Corps, and many of my buddies did exactly that. But the excitement and fulfillment I got during those deployments cemented my decision to stay in. More than ever, the Marine Corps felt like a brotherhood, and I couldn't have been more content.

Ronald Reagan Landing

In the spring of 1988, I had an experience that would change my life—and the course of my career—forever. President Ronald Reagan landed at Air Station Tustin on his way to a fund-raiser in Newport, California.

Steve and I were eager faces in the crowd as seemingly everyone on base stood behind a rope line to watch the squadron arrive. At that time, the Marine Corps was still governed by Cold War policies, so military bases were almost completely off-limits to civilian visitors. It was a purely military crowd gathered at the airstrip, and we had come out in droves to watch the President land.

I had heard of HMX-1, the Presidential Helicopter Squadron One, and the *Marine One* helicopter itself. When I was in OCS at Quantico, where *Marine One* is headquartered, I sometimes saw the white-top helicopters flying in formation to and from the base, but I was too preoccupied with getting through my training to give it much thought.

But now I was witnessing the President's squadron firsthand. First, a couple of sleek helicopters with their tops painted white took turns landing, and some media personnel climbed out. Finally, the very last white-top came in, the one designated *Marine One*. It was obvious that the President was on board from the roar of the cheering crowd around me. At that point in my career, I had worked only with large cargo-type helicopters like the CH-53. I had never seen *Marine One* up close, and I was struck by the nimble movements of the helicopters in formation that seemed almost like an aerial ballet. I was a goner, completely captivated by the choreography of the aircraft hovering and landing in perfect synchronicity.

The President climbed out of the helicopter, waved, and left with his entourage in a motorcade of black limousines. I kept my eyes on the pilots, wearing their dress uniforms with blue pants and khaki shirts, as they milled around their helicopters, apparently waiting for the President to return. They looked so poised and professional, and I knew I was watching the very best of the best. That's when I knew that I wanted to join whatever club they were in.

The week after *Marine One*'s visit, I began to research HMX-1 and inquire about what it took to join the squadron. I learned from a buddy that the group of helicopters used to support the President on any given mission was called the "lift package," and that every single lift was a little different. They landed in a carefully orchestrated formation, specifically planned based on location, weather, wind, and who was on board. I also learned that the Commander of the lift was in charge of making sure that nothing was too predictable and that nobody on the ground could tell which helicopter carried the President, right up until he climbed out. Some call this "the shell game," referring to the old magic trick.

Applying for HMX-1

I wanted to know everything. One of my senior officers in the Red Lions, Major Lee Dial, had been in HMX-1 a few years previously, and was always regaling us with stories of his days in the squadron, carrying President Reagan around the world. I was one of the few pilots who would stick around in the pilots' ready room and listen, enamored with the idea of flying the President.

I did my own research as well, and it wasn't too hard to find the history of HMX-1. The squadron was commissioned on December 1, 1947, at Quantico. The original intent of the Marine Corps' first-ever helicopter squadron was to create an organization focused on developing ways to use helicopters in combat. Within about a year, the squadron conducted the first ship-to-shore helicopter lift in military history. Among numerous other things, HMX-1 developed tactics and techniques that were used very effectively in Vietnam. The pilot fired 2.36-inch rockets that were mounted on the sides of the helicopter and also delivered aerial bombs from up to 8,000 feet.

Throughout the 1950s, the Marines in HMX-1 continued to assess and refine helicopter tactics. The CH-37 and the UH-34 were used extensively during the late 1950s and early 1960s. In September 1957, President Dwight D. Eisenhower was vacationing in Newport, Rhode Island, and flew in a UH-34 back to *Air Force One*. That was the first time a President of the United States had ever flown in a Marine Corps helicopter. President Eisenhower liked the convenience and speed of helicopter travel for short trips, and since then, HMX-1 has provided Executive Support to the President.

As the Executive Support mission evolved, the Marine Corps worked with Sikorsky Aircraft to adopt a special model of the UH-34, called the VH-34. The VH model was equipped with a VIP passenger interior, more-advanced instrumentation, and emergency flotation devices. After a few more iterations, the aircraft was designated the VH-3, an executive version of the Navy's SH-3. The VH-3 was equipped with special soundproofing features, air-conditioning, and even-more-advanced navigational and communications equipment. All in all, the VH-3 provided increased overall safety, reliability, speed, and range. In fact, the style and functionality of the aircraft was so perfect for the mission that it is still in use today.

Since 1947, HMX-1 has supported eleven Presidents and their staffs in more than thirty-three countries, averaging ten thousand flight hours each year. All this has been done in close coordination with Sikorsky. In fact, at one point, an engineer named Harry Asbury noticed that some commercial airlines were painting the tops of their aircraft white to reduce the temperature of the interiors. Rumor has it that the paint upset the pilots and maintenance crews, since it created a lot of extra work and didn't even have a significant impact on the temperature in the cabin. Nevertheless, the "white tops" have persisted, becoming the trademark of *Marine One* for more than five decades.

"White tops," as we call them, are the iconic VH-3 and VH-60 model helicopters authorized to fly the President, the Vice President, the Secretary of Defense, the Chief of Naval Operations, and the Commandant of the Marine Corps. There is no other country, even when they come to the United States, that brings their own helicopter assets. But wherever our Commander in Chief needs to fly, and every time he lands in *Air Force One*, his helicopter is always waiting. The only time a white top is actually referred to as *Marine One* is when the President is on board. With a record free of a single mishap incident, HMX-1 and the white tops have gained a sterling reputation as a truly world-class aviation squadron.

In 1988, I was scheduled to attend a special school called the Weapons and Tactics Instructors Course (WTI), in Yuma, Arizona, to which less than 3 percent of all military aviators are accepted. WTI is an environment not unlike the movie *Top Gun*, except with helicopter pilots, and it took everything I had learned so far to stay ahead of the curve at this level.

Pilots are always given nicknames or radio call signs that everyone tends to use instead of their real names. Every pilot has a different story about how he got his call sign. During this particular course, if you didn't have a call sign—or if the instructors didn't like the one you had—you got a new one. One day I was sitting in a room with other pilots preparing for a flight briefing, and my instructor, a Captain named Jordan Yankov, started asking each of us about our call signs. He took one look at my nametag and said, "No one's ever going to be able to spell that name or pronounce it, so we're just going to call you Frenchy."

Up until that point, I had been given a couple of call signs, like Lash and Rain Man. But none of them had lasted. I wasn't that big of a fan of "Frenchy," but from then on it stuck. Over the years, there were a couple of times when people tried to change my call sign to reflect my passion for fitness and competing in triathlons, but I refused to change it. Jordan had died in an aircraft crash not too long after giving me my call sign, and I kept it in his honor. To this day, there are people I've known for years who don't even know my first name.

Typically, pilots in the Red Lions would do only a couple of overseas deployments in a three- or four-year tour. I had already been to the Western Pacific region on two deployments, which included duty in Okinawa, Japan, and Korea. But when I returned from the WTI course, my commanding officer, Lieutenant Colonel Ned Paulson, asked if I would stick around and do a third deployment. This time it would be Japan and the Philippines, and I happily agreed. Steve had recently been assigned to the Red Lions' higher headquarters, Aircraft Group 16, and had made the decision to leave the Marines at some point to pursue a civilian career. He was right there with me on my first two tours. He had also gotten married while we were stationed in California, and our families spent a lot of time together. It felt strange to deploy without him.

I continued to become a better pilot and became more and more obsessed with the possibility of joining HMX-1. A couple of years after seeing President Reagan land on base, Major Dial was mentoring me through the application process. I had to describe all my training and assignments in detail. I also had to demonstrate through my flight logs that I had flown at least fifteen hundred hours. There were physical and medical requirements as well. I even had to show that I was eligible for a Top Secret clearance. I was advised that a lack of requirements in any of these areas could knock me out of the running, but I felt that I had a pretty good chance. I had received strong performance evaluations in each course, and each year since joining the Red Lions. I was still a young Captain, but I had already gained a great deal of experience.

As if all that wasn't enough, I also needed letters of recommendation, including at least one from someone within HMX-1. The message here was that HMX-1 wanted someone "in the know" to vouch for you, or at least state that they thought you had the potential to thrive at HMX-1. Maybe because he knew how much I wanted the job, Major Dial's recommendation was one of the first that I received. My good friend Marc Hohle had recently left California and entered HMX-1, so I reached out to him and he wrote me a letter as well. I turned in my application packet for HMX-1 in 1991, just before heading out for my third deployment.

I went to Asia, where I worked and flew in the Philippines, in the South China Sea, away from my family, during my last year in the Red Lions.

While I was overseas, Saddam Hussein crossed the border into Kuwait, and the Marine Corps went to war along with the rest of the U.S. military. Operation Desert Shield and then Operation Desert Storm had officially begun, and because of the Marine Corps' stop-loss policy, Steve was deployed to Kuwait for about six months. When he got home, he left the Marines and embarked on a new career in government, but we never lost touch.

I spent the whole war in Japan, and during that time I received news about my HMX-1 application. Command had reviewed it, and I had been selected only as an alternate, which meant that I would not have the opportunity to join HMX-1 for that training year. For me, it was a personal failure. Even though Major Dial and others assured me that it was nothing personal and that I would surely be accepted the next year, it took me a couple of weeks to shake that feeling of failure. It helped when my boss called some of his contacts at HMX-1 and found out that I had been named as an alternate only because I was deployed at the time. They recommended that I apply again the following year, and I learned that alternates are usually a sure thing on their second application.

By 1992 I was already back in the United States and halfway through yet another specialized course—the Amphibious Warfare School (AWS). It was during this school that I was finally accepted into HMX-1. After almost four years of learning all I could about the squadron, submitting two applications, and completing several overseas assignments, I was going to be a pilot in the Presidential Helicopter Squadron! Now we knew we would be in the area for at least five years, so we built a home in nearby Fredericksburg, Virginia.

Spanky got accepted into HMX-1 at the same time, and Bayou would follow us a year later. This was it, and I knew I'd be flying with the best of the best, and in some of the most advanced aircraft in the world.

CHAPTER 3

MY FIRST TOUR

The Big Leagues. The varsity team. I can't believe I'm finally here! These were the thoughts and feelings floating around in my head in the first minutes, hours, and days after arriving at HMX-1 in late May 1992. I rolled up to the main gate of the air facility, deep inside Marine Corps Base Quantico, where a young Marine MP checked my ID, asked the purpose of my visit, and then saluted as I drove off. I knew this was the beginning of a four-year journey unlike anything I had experienced thus far. The Authorization of Deadly Force signs I passed driving to the main HMX HQ building confirmed that. After another vehicle checkpoint, I entered the main compound of HMX-1, that storied organization I had been dreaming about for years now.

I had spent time on Quantico and seen some of the secure areas, but I never had the proper clearances to enter this particular part of the base. I was also accustomed to squadrons that could house their entire staff and aircraft in a single hangar, but this place was huge. It was more of a campus than a hangar.

My buddy Spanky arrived around the same time that day, and we met up and began the week-long process of checking in. First, we went to the Operations Department to hand off our log books and check in with the Operations Duty Officer. This guy was a Captain just like us. And he had a bad attitude. Now, Spanky is not the kind of guy you mouth off to. So, when this Captain did, Spanky asked him very matter-of-factly whether or not he would like a knuckle sandwich.

Spanky looked at me and said, "Great, we've been here less than five minutes and we're going to get into a bar fight!" Both guys stood down, and we continued on to our next stop.

In the Red Lions, I had become a bit of a self-proclaimed expert on HMX-1 history, absorbing all that I could for several years. For example, I knew that this was the largest aviation squadron in the Marine Corps, with a workforce of seven hundred Marines. The pilots, various technicians, and maintenance experts were hand-selected from all over the Marine Corps—they were the best of the best at what they did. But just as a photograph rarely does an ocean sunset justice, my research didn't even come close to preparing me for what this felt like.

We were at the pinnacle of Marine helicopter aviation, and to our fresh eyes it seemed as if half of the workforce was out and about. It was noisy and fast-paced. There were Presidential Seals painted on various signs and I craned my neck to watch as several green-side aircraft and CH-53s flew in pattern above us. A sculptor looks at a block of clay and sees a form hiding inside. As a pilot, I saw the sights and sounds of this exhilarating environment, and saw how I could be part of the history of HMX-1.

One of our next stops was Marine Corps Supply at the other end of the airfield. The young Marine we encountered called the room to attention. I looked behind us to determine what senior officer was sneaking in behind us and then realized, *Holy shit . . . he called the room to attention for us!* We were definitely not in California anymore. The Gunnery Sergeant sitting behind a desk asked us who we were, and then went into a back room to get our supplies.

We had been required to turn in almost all of our gear back at our last commands. We still had some flight suits, but the Sergeant handed over new ones, saying we would need clean ones. I thought that mine were already clean, but apparently they meant *really* clean. My old flight suits had certainly been washed, but it had been so long since I was issued a new one that the hydraulic-fluid stains on mine blended into one color.

We also received a pair of LOX boots. I had no idea what these were at first, or why we were being issued these boots that went only to ankle height and had no laces. We would find out later. For now we just stuffed them into the bag. One thing I had kept from the Red Lions was my flight helmet. Now I had to turn it in for a new one. My helmet had become sort of a friend over the years. I had personally "taped" it up over the years with designs from my old squadron and remembrances from various deployments. I asked why we had to turn in our helmets, and the Gunny stated evenly, "They need to be retaped with the HMX-1 scheme." I reluctantly placed my old friend on the counter.

We were also told to make sure we had a serviceable set of Dress Blue trousers and Service Charlie shirts, which would serve as our official uniform only when flying the white tops on a Presidential lift. This was cool. I was in a whole different league.

We then received four new Squadron patches: one with the HMX-1 insignia, another that was a hybrid of the Presidential Seal and the words "United States Marine Corps Executive Flight Detachment," one with the Presidential Seal, and one with the Vice Presidential Seal. The Gunny informed us that the Presidential and VP patches were for our leather flight jackets, which we would wear during cold-weather lifts. More than any other part of the check-in process, getting these distinctive patches was the most humbling. Who knew how many missions I would wear them on, and who would be in my helicopter? In my own way, I think I knew what a brand-new NFL quarterback must feel like when he is first handed his team's helmet.

We left the supply room and brought our bounty back to our vehicle, securing it all in the trunk. Spanky and I couldn't believe that the Supply Officer was actually handing us all this gear, instead of telling us he had nothing left and to make do with the ratty old gear we had—which often happened in the fleet. We had some other in-processing to do that day, and I also couldn't wait to get down to the hangars and check out the aircraft. We had both seen the airfield before, since we had spent time on Quantico during OCS.

It was still a new experience to get inside the wire and to walk right up to the white tops. The shiny green paint jobs stood out, as did the HMX-1 markings, a far cry from the dirty, hydraulic-fluid stained paint jobs of most fleet aircraft. Along with the white tops (the VH-3 Sea King and VH-60 White Hawk), the HMX-1 fleet includes large cargo helicopters like CH-46s and CH-53s. These platforms participate on Presidential missions but carry only the press, staff, Secret Service, and other supporting personnel.

Over the next couple of days, we checked into other areas of the squadron such as Operations, and met some of our peers as they came on board. We also met the Commanding Officer, Colonel Ed Langston.

On Monday morning, we went into the ready room at 0800. The ready room is the nucleus of daily pilot life, and the heartbeat of HMX-1 operations. Some of the strategic and long-term planning might be done outside that room, but this is where pilots received their daily flight briefs and where All Officer's Meetings (AOMs) were held every morning. In the "normal" fleet, those meetings happened only once a week. It was a fairly plain room with dozens of seats and a big briefing area up front. The most striking things were the pictures on the walls of all the Presidents boarding and coming off HMX helicopters through history.

There was a certain familiarity that is common to all ready rooms in the Marine Corps helicopter community, since the subject matter was helicopters and missions and associated logistics. But the subject matter of the missions was completely new, and that feeling of newness far outweighed my sense of familiarity.

In that first AOM, I was struck by how many pilots across all platforms were there from around the country. I soon realized that our contractors from Sikorsky and Boeing attended these AOMs, along with our Ground Officers, MPs, Supply Officers, the Adjutant, and others. The room was packed with at least fifty people, and half of the HMX-1 pilots were out on missions. Suddenly someone near the back of the room yelled, "Attention on deck!"

We all stopped talking and stood up at the position of attention. Colonel Langston walked in, followed by the Executive Officer, Colonel Mel Demars (who had already been selected to "fleet up" to be the next Commanding Officer). They both walked from the back to the front of the room, and as they did, Colonel Langston said in a very kind voice, "Please be seated." His demeanor was unexpected and very professional. We all sat down. After the Operations Duty Officer conducted the business for that morning's meeting, the CO stood up and faced us from behind a lectern that had the Presidential Seal on it. At the end of his remarks, he said, "We have two new pilots joining us today. Captain Ray 'Frenchy' L'Heureux and Captain Craig 'Spanky' Clement." Each year a new freshman class of pilots came aboard, and we were the latest two of our class to check in. At this introduction, all the other pilots yelled in unison, "Stand up!" We did. The moment we were on our feet, they yelled even louder, "Sit down!" The CO was smiling, and we sat back down, red faced. We were the rookies for the time being, and we knew it.

The CO said, "Welcome," and then it was business as usual. Operations weren't going to slow down or stop until we felt comfortable and understood everything going on. We would just need to catch up and keep up. President Bush 41 had been in office since 1988 and in 1992 was just entering the full swing of campaign mode. The CO said he wouldn't be around that afternoon because he had a meeting at the White House. The President was going out of town for a few days and spending the coming weekend at Camp David. I knew it shouldn't have surprised me, but sitting there hearing that kind of thing blew me away. I had never had anything to do with such high-profile missions back at the Red Lions.

The CO then outlined several current and pending missions, using a whiteboard and some graphics. I felt honored to be working alongside friends from Tustin, like Marc Hohle and Spanky. I even ran into a couple of guys who had been my flight instructors back in Pensacola. The Marine Corps is founded on pride in excellence and esprit de corps, and I had experienced my share of both. But not quite like this. We worked all day, and then on many nights we could actually see the results of our work in the media and in the news. Everyone at HMX-1 seemed to be aware of just how special their jobs were, and everyone seemed extremely proud to be part of this organization. It was contagious. The common denominator was that everyone knew we had a flawless record of achievement, and no one wanted to be the first one in history to change that record.

I had of course read and heard about HMX-1's different missions, but as I settled into the unit, I began to really see how the organization was arrayed. Operationally speaking, there was not only one mission but three, and each one was complex and unique.

The first came from Operational Test and Evaluation (OT&E) and was the reason for the *X* in *HMX*. Back in the early days, when the squadron was formed to develop new helicopter tactics born out of the advent of rotary-wing aircraft and the requirement for that capability in the Korean Conflict, the *X* had stood for *Experimental*. The mission had evolved into the area of testing and evaluation of helicopter systems for use across the Marine Corps. Up until 2011, HMX-1 flew the Operational Test and Evaluation for all rotary-wing aircraft in the inventory. We also tested associated systems such as night-vision goggles, laser eye protection, electronic-warfare equipment, and other flight-physiology-related equipment.

The second mission came directly from the Commandant of the Marine Corps, to the Deputy Chief of Staff for Aviation, to HMX-1. Within this chain of command, we provided helicopter support for various Department of Defense missions, including tactical troop lifts in support of OCS, The Basic School, and Infantry Officer's School. We used the CH-46E Sea Knights, CH-53D Sea Stallions, and CH-53E Super Stallions for these missions.

The most high-profile and unusual mission came directly from the White House—the Executive Transport mission. This was a global mission, meaning that the full contingent of an HMX-1 lift package would be there waiting no matter where the President landed in *Air Force One*. Since President Bush was in campaign mode, the flight schedule was extremely complex and kinetic. We didn't just fly in with a single helicopter. We brought a full lift package wherever we went, and that included a good number of folks for each event site, three or four helicopters, security, maintenance support, and a host of other technicians and communications personnel. Making this seamless involved extremely complex and overlapping logistics and advance planning, as the entire lift package had to be packed up and configured to load onto massive Air Force cargo planes.

From the perspective of the pilots, HMX-1 is set up like a college: you start out as a "freshman" and work your way up to a "senior" during your four-year tour of duty. From the pilots to the crew chiefs, to the maintenance and support personnel, everyone seemed to be at the top of their game. And since you had to be a top gun even to be considered for HMX-1, the pilots jokingly referred to the whole process as going from "hero to zero." For the first year or so, pilots typically serve as Helicopter Aircraft Commander for support aircraft and as copilot for those aircraft during actual Presidential lifts. For the second year, they complete the proper training to become copilots on *Marine One*, which is the whole reason most pilots wanted to join HMX-1 in the first place.

For the last two years of the tour, pilots pretty much end up in one of three categories, each one smaller than the last. The first category is the majority of pilots who are assigned to a supporting role, doing test and evaluation or training missions.

The next category is a little smaller, and fewer than ten of seventy pilots are selected to serve as White House Liaison Officers (WHLOs), which we pronounced "Weelos." This was an important and coveted role because, as the name implied, WHLOs coordinated directly with the White House Communications Office, the Secret Service, the HMX-1 Commander, and numerous other agencies and individuals involved in planning and preparation of the President's movements. Seemingly every one of these entities had its own advance personnel, and the whole group traveled together. The WHLOs were perhaps the most critical component to this overall team, since they arrived in advance, set everything up, and handled the complex logistics of *Marine One*.

The smallest group of pilots in HMX-1 were the four individuals selected by the Commander to fly the President in his absence, or when the logistics of travel made it impossible to keep pace with *Air Force One* around the globe, or simply to fly the other white tops during each Presidential lift. I had to work my way up through these stages just like everyone else.

I was still current in the CH-53, and I began flying again within just a couple of weeks of arriving at the squadron. During this period I also hit my six-year commitment to the Marine Corps, and I didn't consider getting out for even one minute. Some of my peers across the Marine Corps aviation community got out at that point and went into the commercial-aviation industry. Arguably, they could have a lot more personal freedom and make a lot more money on the outside, but I don't recall anyone in HMX-1 getting out for that reason. Yes, I was a freshman, a young Captain, a "zero" finding my way in the juggernaut of a squadron that was HMX-1. But I was also entrusted to fly VIPs in some of the nation's most famous and visible helicopters.

Flying Bush 41

It wasn't long before I began participating in the ongoing support of the President's campaign trail. I wasn't qualified to actually fly President Bush yet, but I flew all over the country with him on support missions. My first full Presidential lift happened a few months into my tour, flying President Bush from the airport in Detroit to a few locations in the area to speak with workers in the automotive industry.

Our squadron arrived in Detroit a couple of days early to rehearse the lift. The stakes are high when the President is on board, and with numerous helicopters taking off and landing in a specific formation, there is no room for error. I understood the mission and knew all the tactics, so I thought I was ready to go on the morning of the lift. I was sitting in the cockpit as the Aircraft Commander of Night Hawk 3, one of four helicopters assigned to the lift package for that day. My big CH-53 would carry members of the President's staff, the press, and the Secret Service.

We were positioned right on the runway, and there were members of the Secret Service, White House staff, and other security all around. I was wearing my official Presidential lift flight suit for the first time. I had almost two thousand flying hours by then, and years of training.

None of that helped me to be any less nervous. I was sweating under my flight jacket despite the morning cold.

I could see the crowd out behind the rope line, not unlike the one I stood behind just a few years before in California. Now here I was walking around freely inside the secure area. I might have been only a pilot on one of the support aircraft on my first Presidential lift, but I was finally in "the club," and that was good enough for me. I talked to some of the other pilots and the Secret Service personnel, but we had to keep our conversations to a minimum. I needed to stay close to the aircraft since we were already in position, waiting for *Air Force One* to arrive.

We monitored several communication channels, the radio crackling with chatter from secure and nonsecure communications, control towers, my Mission Commander (who happened to be the new HMX-1 Commander, Colonel Mel Demars), and the Secret Service. After about a half hour, we got the call on the radio from the WHLO: "Man up . . . *Air Force One* is thirty minutes out."

I climbed back into the cockpit and performed last-minute checks and procedures. I started up the engines, waited for all the other aircraft to get their engines on line, then participated in a quick systems check. *Marine One* then initiated another radio check, and I did not want to miss that one or screw it up in any way. I glanced over at *Marine One*. I could not even fathom the kind of pressure it took to command a flight like that, and what it was like for him to fly with the President of the United States sitting in the back of his aircraft, and perhaps conducting business as the Chief Executive of the United States.

As I watched this gleaming blue-and-white symbol of our country come into view and then touch down, I tried to remind myself, *He's the boss, he's done this dozens of times, he's got this.*

In my imagination, *Air Force One* was a sleek executive jet, not this massive 747 airliner that was now barreling right toward us. The exhaust from the engines made optical illusions in the air around them. This modified 747 was specifically missionized to transport the President of the United States. From talking to other pilots who had toured the aircraft, I knew that *Air Force One* contained a specially outfitted conference room, sleeping quarters, and state-of-the-art communications and security equipment. I would learn later that President Bush 41 was the first President to use this particular aircraft. President Reagan used an older 707, which is now forever parked at the Reagan library.

The jumbo jet kept getting closer and bigger, and I thought that my CH-53 helicopter must look like a metallic bug on the runway. My heart was pumping and my hands were clammy. It was all I could do not to point like a kid pointing at a big yellow jet flying across the sky and say, *Whoa. Look at that!* Once again I tried to play it cool behind my sunglasses while the boy inside me who built that 747 model was going crazy.

For a minute there I thought there had been a mistake, and that they were going to run right over us. Instead, *Air Force One* taxied and rolled to a smooth stop. The wheels were on a predetermined "T" on the ground, which had been precisely measured and marked off by the *Air Force One* advance team. I knew exactly where that spot was, because I had walked out to it and conducted a mental and visual measurement in my head. I had been shocked by how close it seemed to our aircraft. When it finally stopped, security rolled the stairs up to the plane and got to work in a flurry of activity. Then the door opened, and I watched the President step out, wave, walk down the stairs, and greet the staff members, Secret Service personnel, and automotive-industry executives gathered at the bottom.

This was the first time I had seen the President in person. My co-pilot and I just sat there staring fixedly through the cockpit windows, watching the President make his way to Colonel Demars's helicopter. I wouldn't be surprised if our mouths were open. After a couple of minutes, the President and his entourage climbed aboard *Marine One*. Meanwhile, our own passengers climbed on board as well. I had a detailed list of those names approved to be on the flight, and security was extremely tight. I checked the list carefully and ensured everyone was properly buckled in. We usually had seating for twenty-four passengers, but some of the seats were used to hold cameras and other equipment on this flight.

Mary Matalin, a popular news personality, walked on and the whole thing became slightly surreal. Once the President boarded *Marine One*, my Commanding Officer took off. I was still getting our passengers seated and buckled in, so there were a few intense moments as I tried to complete the task, unnecessarily hurrying the ever-competent crew chief in the back. I was nervous, and as soon as I possibly could, I got the rotors turning so I would be ready to take off with the rest of the lift package.

Colonel Demars was all business, and some of us young officers tried to give him a wide berth. It was cold that morning, and I was supposed to be carrying a backup heater and a battery pack in my aircraft that would support the white tops. He knew I didn't have the heater because his crew chief had noticed it in the hangar and grabbed it before we lifted off.

His deep voice came over the radio, "Night Hawk 3, is the auxiliary heating unit on your aircraft?" I froze. Just total radio silence for a few seconds. I looked over at my crew chief in terror. I knew that everyone on the radio was imagining me squirming in my seat, which was pretty accurate.

My crew chief just looked at me with wide eyes and shook his head.

I gulped and prepared to press the Transmit button. The boss was waiting, and I had to say something.

Before I could, the radio crackled again, and Colonel Demars said in a monotone, "The answer would be no."

This became a running joke (they were laughing at me, not with me) for virtually the rest of my time in the squadron.

The sting of being called out over the radio subsided a little when we lifted off. Because *Marine One* took off ahead of us, and my flight needed to land first to get our passengers in place, we increased our speed and passed the President's helicopter, keeping up the shell game as we wove through the Detroit skyscrapers at 200 feet. I had never flown like this before. This was just as amazing as flying over the beach any day. At one point, I saw my own helicopter's reflection on the side of a building and took a quick second to think, *Wow, that is so crazy!* This kind of airspace is normally highly restricted, and loud military aircraft don't typically zoom around the skies of an urban city.

When we arrived at the Ford Motor Company, we landed in the parking lot to a cheering crowd, with camera lights flashing all around us. The President stepped out of *Marine One*, waved at the throngs of people beyond the rope perimeter, and strode into the factory. Sometimes the pilots in a Presidential lift actually get to attend the event, but not this one. We milled around the helicopters, checking all the equipment and waiting for word that the President would be back. That's when we became the celebrities. I was almost embarrassed when people from the local fire and police departments approached us to take pictures with them, and soon the camera flashes were aimed at us. Members of HMX-1 get used to that kind of thing after a while, but it was a new experience for me.

Appointments like this are precisely timed, and we monitored the play-by-play report of the event and its timeline over the radio. Thirty minutes prior to the President's arrival back at the airfield, we would have all aircraft manned with engines running. Finally, the WHLO got the call through his earpiece and relayed to us, "They're wrapping it up. The motorcade is ten minutes out."

We received a similar radio call from the Secret Service at the five-minute mark. We all climbed back into our cockpits with engines running, ready to go. The President and all the other passengers came out of the building and climbed back into the aircraft, and we flew back to the airport. *Marine One* landed last, taxied right up to the nose of *Air Force One*, and discharged the President.

While my passengers were filing out of the helicopter, I had a front-row seat as *Air Force One* turned, accelerated down the runway, then lifted off and flew out of sight. Once it was safely airborne, and the "ramp freeze" was lifted, we taxied to our own "bed down" area on the airport. Next, crews came out to help with cleaning the aircraft and to tow them back into the hangar. We debriefed the flight, then went back to the hotel and changed clothes. *Mission complete!*

Though it still felt like one, the experience had been more exciting than any daydream. I couldn't quite believe that this was now my job. When I got back to the hotel, I immediately called my wife, then my parents, then Steve, and probably a few others. I probably sounded like a kid, "Did you see me on TV?" Of course they hadn't, but the exhilaration of that relatively short lift had left me with a strong desire to turn around and do it all again.

Walleyball? With the President?

Later in 1992, I got to meet President Bush 41 up close. We flew the President and First Lady to Camp David—my first official trip to the Presidential retreat that sits 2,300 feet above sea level in the beautiful wooded hill country of Maryland. Because Camp David is run by the Navy, when the First Family is not there it's quite like any other military installation—except for the fact that it sits beneath a dome of highly prohibited airspace.

I had been to the camp a couple of times in a training capacity, but now the Boss was on the lift and the pressure and excitement grew exponentially. By helicopter, the trip from the White House lasts about forty-five minutes, and is fairly technical and challenging. This was a mountainous area, and it was difficult to spot the landing zone cut out from the dense trees until we were fairly close. It was beautiful to fly in so low over the trees in the morning sun, but I kept my mind focused on the task at hand.

Not unlike the approach to the White House lawn, the small clearing in the trees below did not seem large enough to land the lift package. But of course it was. We finally landed and shut down the engines. The landing zone was actually a large grassy area that doubled as a skeet-shooting and driving range when the First Family was in residence. It was obvious that Camp David had been readied for the First Family's arrival—flags flying in the wind, with Marines and Sailors standing at attention or saluting in their crisp dress uniforms. The President, the First Lady, and a few of their grandchildren climbed out of *Marine One* and into the prestaged golf carts waiting for them at the top of the landing zone. We watched them drive off and then began to do final checks and preparations to button up the aircraft before they were towed to the hangar. No matter what, care and maintenance of the aircraft was always a top priority.

Pilots are considered guests at Camp David, since they have to stay there as long as the President is there and must be ready to leave on a moment's notice. We were technically on duty all weekend. Camp David is officially known as Naval Support Facility Thurmont. It was originally designed as a camp for military officers and their families; then President Franklin Delano Roosevelt turned it into his Presidential retreat and named it Shangri-La. President Eisenhower later changed the name to Camp David, after his grandson. The place is meticulously maintained all year and kept lush and green, with wide open spaces and shaded trails connecting the buildings where camp employees work and live. Not surprisingly, Camp David is well equipped.

You can find anything there that one would expect at a military facility: barracks for the Marines and Sailors, guest cottages, dining halls, even a gym and small movie theater.

We put the aircraft in the hangar and then received a quick briefing about the weekend plans and schedule. My buddy Mike Manzer, another copilot, drove me over to the pilots' cabins in a golf cart. It was called Walnut, and it was furnished like a hotel, with two bedrooms, TVs, and a private bathroom.

That evening, the military aide called Mike and said, "Hey, the Boss wants to play walleyball, and he wants to play with the Marines. Be down at Wye Oak gym at 1600."

He stopped by my cabin and gave me the news.

"'Walleyball'?" I asked.

"Yeah, it's volleyball, but on a racquetball court. And the President is damn good at it."

A short golf-cart ride later, I was standing in a racquetball court with a net running the width of it. The courts were inside the gym, which was a beautiful facility housing basketball courts, a swimming pool, a sauna, and a weight room. It was designed by Arnold Schwarzenegger when he served as Bush 41's Chairman of the President's Council on Physical Fitness and Sports. As I stood there with other pilots, the military aide, and a couple of the ubiquitous Secret Service guys, President Bush walked onto the court smiling and said, "Hey, fellas, how you doing?" He was wearing a T-shirt, shorts, and tennis shoes. It was the first time I had ever seen him out of a suit.

I managed to say, "Great, sir."

He was tall and athletic, smiling as he shook our hands. Being that close to the President of the United States for the first time—and knowing that I was about to compete against him—was a little intimidating. Once we started, though, we became just a bunch of guys playing a game.

This was my first time playing walleyball, and being a pretty competitive person, I decided to do my best, but there was no way I was going to spike the President! Alex Gierber, one of the copilots playing that day, was a huge Argentinean guy who probably stood six feet tall and weighed 250 pounds. He was playing right up on the net, directly across from President Bush. The game was moving fast, and I could tell that Alex had the same concerns that I had. He'd had a couple of opportunities to really smash the ball, but he was holding back.

Then the President grabbed up the ball and said, "Hold up. Hold up, guys." He looked Alex square in the eyes and grinned. "Look, son, if you're not going to play the game, I can get somebody in here that will." It was like he was saying, *Don't you go easy on me. I can take it.*

Alex is one of those people you have to tell only once. And sure enough, within the next couple of volleys, he stuffed the President pretty good. The President's glasses were hanging askew and he lost his balance a bit. Everyone froze, especially on our side of the net. A second later I could hear the Secret Service guys chuckling.

President Bush stood up, straightened his glasses, looked at Alex again, and said, "Now that's what I'm talking about." The game picked up again, and eventually the President said, "Okay, that's it for me. Thanks for the fun and the exercise and I'll catch you later," while wiping the sweat off his forehead with a towel. I managed to stay cool until the President headed back to his cabin.

I made some excited phone calls to family and friends when I got back to my cabin that night. I spent the rest of the weekend reading, working out, and eating at the chow hall. On Saturday night it was nearing dusk and I was playing horseshoes outside the cabins with a couple of the other pilots. As the sun dropped behind the mountain and it really started getting dark, we were starting to finish up our game.

Barbara Bush was walking nearby with her grandchildren, whom they had brought on the trip. As she passed within about twenty feet of us, she looked in our direction and said, "Who is that over there bangin' up George's shoes?"

We laughed and said, "Ma'am, it's just us, the Marines."

She said, "Okay then, before one more horseshoe gets thrown, it's getting cold out and you all better put on jackets."

We all said, "Yes, ma'am, of course," and we knew the game was over. It was getting too dark anyway. I still don't know for sure if that was her subtle way of telling us to stop banging horseshoes or if she was actually concerned that we were going to get cold. On Sunday evening we flew the First Family back to D.C., and I was once again blown away by the types of things I did in a day's work at HMX-1. The First Family always treated us wonderfully up there at Camp David, and everywhere else for that matter.

These were some of the best years of my life. I was participating in the most unusual and exciting missions, and learning so much. We lived in Fredericksburg, Virginia, and Ray Jr. and Delia were around nine and ten during this period. While I worked fifty to sixty hours a week, and traveled quite often, my wife handled everything at home. Thanks to her, the kids were doing great and thriving in school, soccer, band, and other activities. Steve was busy in his new career, but we kept in close contact. He even spent a couple of weekends at our house when he was in the area, and I had the opportunity to show him around HMX-1 a bit.

On "normal" weekends, when enough of us "locals" were in town, we would plan family barbecues, birthday parties, dinners—any excuse to get together and have some fun. Spanky bought a home in southern Stafford, Virginia, and I remember thinking it was the biggest house I'd ever seen for a single guy. Spanky has that MacGyver gene, and he can fix anything. He did a lot of the work on the house himself, including the planning and construction of a hot tub and a bar on the back deck. His house became the nexus of our social activities. The bar became affectionately known as the Beach Bongo Belly Up Bar, and it even featured a thatched roof. About a year after Spanky and I arrived, Bayou finally showed up and took his usual place in our ongoing professional and personal adventures.

President Bush Departs and President Clinton Comes on Board

President Bush and his family treated all of us like gold, and we supported them proudly. It was as if our intimate connection with the President made him not only our boss but almost a father figure. During the Presidential elections of November 1992, the country really was polarized by the differences between President Bush 41 and Presidential candidate Bill Clinton (not unlike the polarity we would experience later with Bush 43 and Obama), but we all assumed President Bush 41 would win the election.

Instead, we woke up to learn that we were going to serve a forty-second President, Bill Clinton. I had been in HMX-1 for only about a year, but the overwhelming feeling was that of a favorite coach being replaced. Over the next few months we were in state of transition and preparation for the incoming administration.

In January 1993, we had to say farewell to President Bush. As chance would have it, I was off duty and not required to fly during President Clinton's Inauguration Ceremony. Instead, I watched on a TV at Quantico as my Commanding Officer at the time (Colonel Ed Langston) flew President Bush on a victory lap over the National Mall. I knew that while the Colonel's relationship with the President was kept purely on a professional level, he had a deep respect for his boss. I could only imagine how he felt giving his Commander in Chief one last ride to honor and thank him.

Although we maintained the highest professionalism during the transition from Bush 41 to Clinton, it was a major adjustment both operationally and emotionally. It was during this time that I really began to appreciate how apolitical being a White House pilot was. It didn't matter if you agreed personally with a President's political standing or policies. He was the Commander in Chief, and you had to provide the same world-class support at all times.

Still somewhat of a new guy, I just did my job and watched the chaos of the transition unfold. Bush 41 was very punctual and always had a detailed calendar of events. As a result, the squadron had become accustomed to an orderly, well-thought-out travel plan. Naturally, with an entirely new (and very young) staff replacing an experienced one, things were not nearly as organized or predictable.

I remember one story that makes the point real: The first time HMX-1 flew President Clinton, nobody on his staff briefed him on the protocol for saluting as he boarded *Marine One*. There is always a Marine standing at the base of the stairs of *Marine One*, and he salutes the Commander in Chief. Of course, the President is supposed to salute the Marine back and then put his arm down. For some reason, he just boarded the aircraft without saluting. This created some confusion for the Marine and a generally awkward moment. Since this was Clinton's first time in *Marine One*, there was a lot of press coverage and the moment was captured on TV. The media ate it up, and it became a major topic of discussion for a while there. Half of the media outlets stated how shameful and disrespectful it was, and the other half said it was a simple mistake, while correspondents and military advisers chimed in on the issue.

Internally, we figured he simply hadn't been briefed. He had never been in the military and was not familiar with our customs and courtesies. No big deal. Over time, that little incident blew over and it did not happen again. Operations settled into a smoother rhythm, and I served as a Presidential copilot flying President Clinton all over the planet. The Clintons didn't own a home anywhere, so when they were away from the White House they were either at Camp David or with friends. For example, I flew them to Martha's Vineyard once, to spend a weekend with Warren Buffett. Because of my job in HMX-1, I often accompanied them on these trips and came to see that the Clintons were extremely kind and grateful toward the military, not unlike President Bush 41 and his family.

Over the course of my career, I would land on the White House lawn countless times, and it was almost always in the Sea King. I'll never forget the first time, which was during a Presidential lift not long after Clinton's inauguration. The First Lady's father had passed away, so the President was returning from the memorial services that had been held in Arkansas. Due to weather concerns, on the way out he had gone from the White House to Andrews AFB in his motorcade. *Marine One* was scheduled to pick him up at Andrews and bring him home this evening.

I had recently completed my saturation training, and Colonel Langston had selected me as his copilot for this lift. I had already been part of a few lifts, and even commanded support aircraft, but now I was going to copilot *Marine One* itself, with the President on board! I had also flown past the White House a number of times, but had never taken that right turn toward the South Lawn. This was going to be another brand-new experience, but one that I had already played out in my mind many times.

Everyone was well aware that because the copilot was in the left seat, the same side of the aircraft as the air stair, the copilot usually showed up in all the official photographs. In fact, pilots teased one another about this phenomenon, and sometimes made a point to stare at the White House after landing. When it worked out and we found the shot later on one of the media sites, we passed it around the ready room and jokingly called it the Geek of the Day photo. This was going to be a night landing, so there wouldn't be those kinds of photos, and I certainly wouldn't be the Geek of the Day.

Earlier in the day, we took the aircraft up for a test flight, and to burn off some fuel so that conditions were just perfect when we picked up the President. Now it was go time. It was a breezy evening when I walked out to the flight line with Colonel Langston, both of us wearing our formal lift uniform and leather flight jackets. We climbed aboard and began preparing the aircraft for our mission, following every step precisely. We started the engines, called the control tower, and received clearance for the flight.

The trip from Anacostia to Andrews AFB takes only a few minutes, but there is an invisible maze of restricted airspace that you cannot see using the natural landmarks in the area. We landed at Andrews just in time, and waited for *Air Force One* to arrive with the President. Within minutes, *Air Force One* landed, the President boarded *Marine One*, and we received clearance to lift off once more.

We gained altitude and turned toward the nearby Potomac River. Easing up to 200 feet, we turned to the northwest and followed the river. I immediately noticed that there was no moon, but a number of stars were out. The Potomac was nothing more than a dark line threading between two black horizons, its glassy surface reflecting the lights of the structures near its banks. The sunlight that usually lit the cockpit had now been replaced by the ambient light of the backlit controls. I had to call upon my training in an entirely different way to monitor and manipulate the panel of green and yellow indicator lights and gauges floating between me and the night sky. This was more intense than any video game. This was true point-of-view game play, virtual reality that included all five senses.

As copilot, I had a great deal of responsibility, such as making radio calls, overall navigation, choreographing the other aircraft in the lift, and giving the pilot all the visual cues he needed throughout the flight. There's a specific spot on the Potomac where you can turn right in between the two prohibited areas, one being over the White House, the other being over the Naval Observatory where the Vice President lives.

When we approached the right spot, I called the National Tower: "*Marine One.* Three minutes out."

The tower knew what I meant, and granted us permission.

We neared the Washington Monument, adorned in its nightly gown of white light. I again called for clearance as Colonel Langston put the monument on our right and started our final approach to the South Lawn. I knew that I was flying low over streets and suburbs, but at that moment it was a constellation of lights below that challenged me to stay focused on the most important lights of all—the ones straight ahead. The White House looked like a miniature version of itself all glowing with soft white light. The South Lawn was not lit, but I could see the vague shape of the fountain, as small as a toy in the darkness below us.

Our landing lights broadened our visibility as we moved closer, exposing the details I needed to guide Colonel Langston in. I was humbled by the Colonel's finesse as he flew us into what seemed like a black hole. I helped him to stay clear of the trees on the left. Finally, I could clearly see the three six-foot-long red disks that we needed to land on. The disks were used to ensure the same landing spot each time, and to protect the manicured lawn.

Colonel Langston's pedal turned the aircraft to the left, while turning the nose to the right, as if he were squeezing into a tight parking space. Now the White House was on our left. The pilot can only see directly in front of him, so I had a much better view of the disks by looking out to the left of the cockpit. I knew that if we put the front-left landing gear on the center of the front-left disk, and if Colonel Langston kept the aircraft straight, then all three landing gears should be right on target.

As we hovered ten feet off the ground, then five, I gave him instructions: "A little forward. A little left. You're good." Not surprisingly, he had deftly maneuvered the Sea King in between those dark and protective trees and made a perfect landing. Trying to control my oscillating sense of accomplishment and complete childish glee, I realized how very few people would ever get the chance to land on this spot of earth.

Making the moment even more memorable, President Clinton came up into the cockpit before climbing off the aircraft. He thanked us for the flight, and I turned sideways in my seat so that I could see him better. Knowing that our passengers had just attended the memorial services, Colonel Langston looked him right in the eye and said, "Sir, all of the Marines of HMX-1 are very sorry for your loss." He remained in the cockpit for about five minutes, and in the night outside the aircraft, I could see the Secret Service getting a little antsy.

I knew that life in Washington, D.C. went on below us. Couples were perhaps finishing up a late dinner after a long day at work, while parents tucked in their kids or watched TV. My family was nearby in Fredericksburg, doing the same. And as they did, we lifted off and headed back to Anacostia, talking about the President's kind words in the cockpit.

Besides my heightened sense of awareness (and nervousness), I was acutely aware of how Colonel Langston handled himself. I knew that he had recently flown President Bush on his victory lap, after serving as his pilot for several years. With about six months to go in his tenure as CO, he had just flown a new President for the first time. I couldn't have predicted it then, but years later I would find myself in the same situation as Colonel Langston, when I flew President Obama for the very first time.

A couple of weeks later, I had my first daytime landing on the

White House lawn. This time I was copilot for one of the Command Pilots, Major Jay Anderson, and we were going to pick up the President and fly him to Delaware. In some ways, the day landing was much like the nighttime landing. Same time frame, same control of the aircraft, same goal. In another sense, it was an utterly different sensory experience.

After lifting off just as I had with Colonel Langston, the Washington Monument loomed in the distance. I had stood at its base with my family when we first moved to the area, shielding our eyes from the sun and looking up toward the top. At over 500 feet tall, the monument now towered over our helicopter as we came in at 200 feet. Jay made precise adjustments to maintain a very specific distance from the monument. Once again I called on the radio to receive final clearance to approach the White House and land on the South Lawn. This was far away from those grassy fields in Pensacola where I first learned how to hover.

If I could snap a mental picture and freeze-frame it for a just a moment, this is what I would have seen: to my left, treetops and houses spanning out for miles. To my right, the Washington Monument and the Potomac, and a sea of trees beyond that. Below me, busy city streets and intersections. People were driving and walking around, some looking up at the helicopter that might or might not be carrying their President. And straight ahead, the White House itself, more white and vivid than any photograph I had ever seen. More gleaming and patriotic than I had even expected. But I did not stop to enjoy the view. I just scanned and processed all those sights. I remained alert and present.

The South Lawn looked tiny, blocked in by large trees, and the fountain seemed to be placed right up against the building. I marveled that Colonel Langston had made it look so easy, even in darkness. There seemed not to be enough room to fit our helicopter in there, but as we moved in closer, my depth perception moved right along with me. The grass was startlingly green and the trees seemed way too close, but I realized that there was ample room for a very precise maneuver. I couldn't help but remind myself that all the trees towering over the South Lawn, flailing their branches and leaves in the wind, had been planted by former Presidents.

Seeing the White House from this angle had me a little nervous. Thought after thought bounced around in my brain as I used my training to be the best copilot I possibly could be. I guided the pilot in for a precise landing, and this time the press was there in full force. I found myself looking toward the White House as the President came out and walked to the helicopter, and I wondered if someone was snapping my picture. We flew the President to the event in Delaware and then flew him back home. Put it down in the book: it was yet another great day to be part of HMX-1.

President Clinton used Camp David as a retreat the least of all the Presidents I flew. Still, I did take him and Mrs. Clinton to Camp David a couple of times. One day, we picked them up at the White House, and as always, the First Lady said good morning as she climbed the stairs while holding Chelsea's hand. Once we landed them on camp and settled into the cabins, the military aide called and said we had been invited to join the First Family in the theater. The film happened to be *Starship Troopers*, which is about a futuristic Marine unit.

I sat right behind the Clintons with another pilot, and as the film began, the President turned around and asked if we wanted any popcorn. The President asked *us* if we wanted popcorn.

"Sure thing, sir."

At one point in the movie, the Marines were firing these fictitious weapons called Morita MK 1s, which seemed to work pretty well on humans but weren't working all that well on the arachnids. The President turned around and said, "How would you guys like some of those?" then chuckled.

I was hoping he meant the guns and not the spiders. "Ha-ha . . . uh . . . yes, sir," we both mumbled. I mostly sat there mesmerized, my eyes drifting down from the screen to the three heads in front of me. I was watching a movie about a futuristic battle against alien bugs where the humans were fighting for survival with guns that didn't seem to be working all that well on the bugs, while the President of the United States and his family were sitting right in front of me and we were all eating popcorn.

This was no regular night at the local Cineplex.

With Pope John Paul II in the Passenger Seat

While I was becoming accustomed to flying precious cargo and had now been a Presidential copilot for some time, nothing prepared me to fly Pope John Paul II in 1993. He was in the United States for World Youth Day in Denver, Colorado, and I felt like I had won the lottery when I was selected as the copilot for the mission. HMX-1 doesn't usually fly anyone except the President and his staff outside the D.C. Beltway—except the Pope. I spoke to Bayou and Spanky the day before the lift, and they teased me about being the lucky one to get selected. Lucky or not, I was just happy to have the opportunity.

My family is very, very Catholic. To them, carrying the Pope held a lot more water than carrying the President. My grandmother was a blue-blooded Bostonian Catholic, and in her opinion the Pope could do no wrong. She even said, "The heck with Clinton. You're flying the Pope, I can die now."

As usual, we showed up early to coordinate the landing site, security, and the multitude of other concerns. Not only were we supporting the Pope's visit, but President Clinton was also coming to Denver to meet with the Pope, so HMX-1 had a very strong presence in the area. In the days preceding the Pope's visit, there was a palpable electricity in the air. There were police, security personnel, people from the Catholic Diocese, Cardinals, and Bishops getting everything ready. We went out to dinner in town in the evenings, and there were peddlers everywhere selling Pope-related memorabilia like the poetically named Pope Scopes, which were like little plastic periscopes you could use to see the Pope from within the massive crowd.

When the Pope actually arrived, we were positioned at Stapleton International Airport, and I watched this huge Alitalia Airlines jet land and taxi up to us. It's one thing to see the President walking down the steps of *Air Force One* toward you, but this was a completely different kind of feeling. This went beyond professional and entered into the personal. This was the Pope, and when he climbed on board, I felt his powerful presence. I remember feeling like, *This is probably as close to God as I'm ever going to get.* There were a few days before World Youth Day, and the Pope didn't motorcade anywhere. Since the President was not on board, and the Pope was considered a head of state, the call sign for the day was "State One." We flew in State One to schoolyards, monasteries, and parks, and each time there was a swarm of security, Vatican personnel, and onlookers.

When the day of the event arrived, we flew the Pope right over the rim of Mile High Stadium before landing in a secure location. I had to imagine that there was a security blanket over the entire state of Colorado, and every radar in the world probably had a pinpoint location on where we were. After all, we were carrying the leader of one of the largest faiths in the world. As we flew up over the lip of the stadium, one of the other aircraft had already gone ahead of us, and I heard the crowd going wild. We cleared the rim and I saw the largest crowd I had ever flown over at that point in my life.

There was a sea of people in the stands and on the field who had descended on Denver for the event. I had never even landed a President in a crowd this big. Tens of thousands of people stood and cheered in pockets of color, representing their countries by wearing uniforms that matched their flags. Throngs of Nuns, Bishops, and security personal swarmed among them. The other helicopters carrying the Vatican staff landed first, so they could get into position. We finally landed and the Pope got off and into the Popemobile, a modified vehicle that looked like a high-end golf cart encased in bulletproof glass.

You never know if you'll be invited into an event, and most of the time we weren't. But we were invited into this one, so, after securing the aircraft, I walked through the crowd with my buddy Mike Sparr, who is one of the funniest people I've ever met in my life. We found a spot right at the base of the huge statue of a bronco, and we had a pretty decent view overlooking the stage. I noticed that Mike had little vials of water in all his pockets, which he hoped to get blessed by the Pope.

I said, "You better hope you don't fall down. You'll look like you pissed your pants."

He said, "Don't worry about me. I have a hundred bucks' worth of lottery tickets right here," as he patted his left breast pocket. "If it's going to happen, it's going to happen now."

When the Pope took the stage, we could barely see him amid the sea of Pope Scopes. The energy of the place was palpable, and I was inspired to have the honor of watching and hearing the Pope speak that day. Thirty minutes before the event ended, the WHLO alerted us to prep the aircraft. We quickly made our way back to the landing zone. When the event was over and the Pope made his way back to the aircraft, he presented two young Marines with a pair of blessed rosary beads and papal coins. They were grateful to say the least. We lifted off from Mile High Stadium and flew the Pope to a couple more events that day, including a meeting with President Clinton.

The next day, we flew him to a Catholic retreat called Saint Malo's, way up in the Rocky Mountains. The plan was that he would relax there for the weekend before his last event on Sunday. We jokingly called the event "Popestock" because there were supposed to be half a million people at a place called Cherry Creek Park for Sunday Mass.

The weekend retreat was not one of those trips where we fly the VIP or person to the destination and then fly away. The staff wanted us there so that if anything happened, we could get the Pope out of there quickly. The place was empty that weekend except for the Pope, close Vatican staff, Secret Service, the resort staff, and us HMX-1 personnel. We all got to meet the Pope, and he gave us rosary beads. When we met, I shook his hand, and he asked me a few questions. When I answered his questions, he usually smiled and said, "I bless your families."

He also decided to go on a hike at one point and invited us to join him. When I showed up at the appointed time and place for the hike, the Pope was still wearing his garments, but instead of the typical headgear he was wearing a white driver's cap, the same kind that the cartoon character Andy Capp used to wear. He reminded me of my grandfather.

When we flew the Pope to Cherry Creek Park for Sunday Mass, I quickly added that day to the growing list of my most memorable experiences. We got a call from the Vatican staff, saying that they wanted to put a video guy in the back of the aircraft and record the Pope as we circled the park before landing. The video of the Pope waving down at the crowd would be instantly transmitted to the JumboTrons set up on both sides of the stage. We had never done that before but got approval to do it for the Pope. As usual, we landed in a predetermined spot behind the stage, and then the Pope got out and climbed into a Winnebago. When he emerged, he was dressed in his vestments for celebrating Mass, and I had another opportunity to interact with him. All the pilots were standing in a kind of receiving line with other people who had been allowed backstage.

Right next to me was a little girl in a wheelchair with her mother. I could tell that the little girl had a severe case of muscular dystrophy, and there were several other ill children beside them. As the Pope made his way down the line, looking everyone in the eye and shaking their hands and speaking a few words of blessing, the little girl's mother had tears streaming down her face. I was overcome by emotion myself, as I could only imagine the challenges this woman had overcome and how meaningful it must have been for her to be in the presence of the Pope. The Pope said a few words to me, and I was again enthralled by his energy, and then he got down on one knee in front of the crippled girl as her mother sobbed.

He took the little girl's hands into his and bowed his head. The mother was sobbing hysterically now, clearly overcome with hope and releasing all the pain she'd built up. He then stood up, took the little girl's face in his hands, and then took the mother's hands, and blessed them both. Her display of raw emotion had just about everyone crying, even us tough Marines.

He got up onto the stage and delivered a wonderful Mass, and I heard the massive crowd just going nuts. During the Mass, his words were being translated into different languages. Once the event was over, we flew him back to the airport for his flight back to Rome. But before he boarded his plane, he was scheduled to meet with Vice President Al Gore. From our perspective, Vice President Gore was always very stoic and rarely had anything to say to us. Since he didn't display much congeniality with us, we never really formed a bond with him. He certainly never asked or offered to take pictures with us.

But apparently this day was different. As the pilots were taking a photograph with members of the Denver Police Department, the Pope came over to thank us one last time and to get in the picture. To our surprise, Vice President Gore came over and joined the photo. In my humble opinion, he would never have done that if the Pope had not been there.

The Pope boarded his aircraft, and the events in Colorado were complete. We were all very pleased with our performance in supporting the Pope and the President and how unusual the whole experience had been. I got back to the hotel room and immediately called my parents and grandmother to tell them all the details I knew they were expecting. When I told them about the Pope blessing the little girl backstage, and the speech at World Youth Day, and the hike up at Saint Malo's, they were proud of me, a member of the Marine Corps who flew with the Pope.

White House Liaison Officer (1995–1996)

Before long my second year was almost finished, and it was time for another phase within HMX-1. Although I did perform well, at the time there were a lot of other qualified pilots who had more seniority than I had. I was still a Captain, and there was an abundance of qualified Majors. I knew that the math just wasn't working in my favor, and resigned myself to the fact that I could still fly the Vice President and still copilot a Presidential lift, but I was not going to be one of the four command pilots serving right under the HMX-1 Commander. I was okay with that, because more than anything, I wanted to be one of the eight pilots selected as a WHLO. It's one of the most unusual jobs in HMX-1 and in the Marine Corps in general. I also knew that as a WHLO, in certain situations I would represent and make decisions on behalf of the HMX-1 Commander in the field. I felt like I was up for that challenge, and saw it as an opportunity.

I was selected, and I spent the last two years of my tour as a WHLO. During that time, I traveled to several countries, and sometimes literally at the last moment. My flight time dropped because I was always on the road, but when I was in town, the operations section made sure I got time in the cockpit. More than anything, being a WHLO made me an expert in HMX-1 planning and logistics, and it was by far the most responsibility I had ever had or dreamed of having.

My mentor and friend Willie Willard (former CO of the Red Lions) was working at Naval Air Systems Command and living in Springfield, Virginia. Every couple of months he invited us up for a Sunday barbecue. I was up for promotion to Major, and the small ceremony would take place on December 1, 1995. Promotion or "pinning" ceremonies are among many traditions in the Marine Corps. Usually my Commanding Officer would promote me, but you always had the option of requesting that someone else stand in at the ceremony. I asked Colonel Demars if he would be okay with Willie promoting me, and he said, "Absolutely."

I then asked Willie if he would promote me, and he readily agreed. Willie is one of those great orators who can speak off-the-cuff, while injecting hilarious anecdotes and fun into his speeches. Again, it was a very small ceremony, with my family and a couple of my buddies. Willie made a few remarks and a few jokes as my expense, then placed my new rank on my uniform. It was another of countless proud moments for me.

I am always shocked when I see myself, as a member of HMX-1, through my family's eyes. I was still just the same old Ray, but when my family saw me in the line of duty, I realized on an even more profound level just how incredible my job was. During the midterm elections of 1995, President Clinton was traveling to Manchester, Nashua, and some other areas near my hometown. One of those stops was Franklin, New Hampshire, which was only about thirty miles from my parents' home.

Steve "Cujo" Cusomano was with me, as I was training him on WHLO activities, and we were in a local hotel for the event. Following standard procedure, we arrived a couple of days early to start coordinating the trip. One night we drove down to my parents' house for dinner, then went out for a few drinks with my brothers. As a WHLO, we always checked out the restaurants and businesses in the local area, but this was different. This was my old stomping ground. I showed Cujo where I had gone to school and one of the restaurants where I had worked, and we ended up at a new microbrewery that seemed to pop up amid a string of nationwide microbreweries. We sampled some of the local brew, relaxed, and listened to the live band. My brother Roger, a musician through and through, pulled out his harmonica and started jamming with the band. I had seen him do this so many times I'd lost count, but Cujo thought it was simply amazing. Instead of going back to our hotel, I crashed in my parents' spare bedroom and Cujo crashed on the couch.

The next morning we had to get out to the airfield early and coordinate the lift package with law enforcement and the Secret Service. We had to blend in, so we were wearing suits and ties, not our Marine uniforms. Once we got down to the site, we secured the rope line, and my wife, parents and in-laws were there among the crowd of faces, not unlike the time Steve and I first saw President Reagan land back in Tustin. But now I was the suited Marine moving around and making arrangements within the secure area of the airfield. I talked to the Secret Service guys, coordinated with the aircraft on the radio, and when the *Marine One* lift package finally came into view and approached us, I choreographed the landing perfectly. This was the first time my family had seen me working in person like this, and I'd be lying if I said I didn't steal a look or two over at them, and that I didn't enjoy the immense look of pride in their eyes. After the President landed, another rare opportunity made the day even more memorable.

Just because *Marine One* happens to be in your hometown, and just because you happen to be a WHLO, that doesn't mean you're guaranteed to have your family meet the President. In fact, it's highly unlikely. Well, it was one of my lucky days. As the President made his way to the rope line to shake hands and meet with the locals, I asked the military aide over the radio if he thought the President might want to take a picture with the family of one of his HMX-1 WHLOs.

The aide spoke to the President, then came back on the radio and said yes, that would be fine. He then asked me where they were standing, and told me to head over in that direction. I made my way to the rope line and stood next to my family before the President got there. The President walked up to us, with his Secret Service guys all around, said "Hi, Major," and then kindly offered to take the picture. I said, "Thank you, sir," after the camera went off and he began to move down the rope line. My mother-in-law was a big Clinton fan, so she was completely enamored. In real time, the moment lasted only a few seconds, but in the memory of my family, the moment will go on forever.

The Fiftieth Anniversary of D-day

In 1994, I was one of the WHLOs assigned to the advance team during President Clinton's visit to Normandy, France, for the fiftieth anniversary of D-day. I arrived early to coordinate all the logistics, landing zones, schedules, and security surrounding *Marine One*'s support of the President. I had never been to France at that point, and since joining HMX-1 it was my first time traveling overseas as a member of the advance team.

I had been in Europe for seventeen days when the President arrived. His trip began in Naples and included Rome and Paris before ending in Normandy. After a few days of traveling around just hundreds of feet above the European countryside, we arrived in Calais, which is a little seaside town next to Normandy.

The city was completely electrified with activity, and there were WW II veterans all over the place. On my downtime, I walked the streets, just taking in the scene and talking to some of the local towns-people. It didn't take me long to realize that the people living in the region remembered what had happened. They never forgot the fact that the United States and its allies had liberated France. It was a very important part of their history, and for the fiftieth anniversary, many homes proudly flew American and French flags side by side.

One day I was out with some other Marines on the advance team, some Secret Service guys, some Air Force guys, and a couple of White House staffers. There were little cafés and pubs all over the place, and they were all teeming with patrons. While having a drink inside one, we struck up a conversation with some old retired Army guys. One of them in particular was very talkative, and I was humbled and amazed by the fact that they had actually landed on those beaches in 1944, and survived, and now here they were back in Normandy fifty years later to remember the occasion.

I said, "Sir, can I buy you a beer?"

He started laughing at me and said, "Son, you start that, and you're going to have to buy this whole event a beer and you can't do that. So tell you what, let me buy you a beer instead."

I was stumped. These guys had stormed the beaches of Normandy, and now they were thanking us for our service and buying us a beer!

Later during the trip, my Commanding Officer flew President Clinton to the American cemetery that overlooks Omaha Beach. It's located in Colleville-sur-Mer, and almost 9,400 people are buried there. Since the cemetery is actually U.S. Park territory, we are the only helicopters that can land our head of state ceremonially right there at the cemetery.

As I watched President Clinton speak to the crowd on that cloudy day in June, I was moved by the history of what had happened in that place, the survivors standing all around me, the dead buried row on row. That I was part of it all made me even more proud to be an American than I usually am.

•   •   •

I stayed busy, spending time at home when I was in town, coordinating Presidential lifts all over the country, and making several overseas trips as well. Although the Clintons definitely treated the Marines of HMX-1 very well, sometimes we were still reminded of how great President Bush's organized schedule had been. In early 1996, I was in Rhode Island planning a lift, and I received a call from HQ.

"Frenchy, you're the last guy available. The President just added Cairo to his Israeli trip, and you need to go there. Now."

"Right now?" I said. "When will the President arrive?"

"If you leave now, you might have about ten to twelve hours before the lift package arrives," he said.

Now I knew this was serious. Usually, I would have days or even weeks to coordinate a trip. I was already way behind the power curve. I packed up my suitcase and went straight down to the airport, where my reservation was waiting for me. This had all happened so quickly, I had no idea who was going to meet me there. After the first leg of the trip, I had to switch to an Egyptair plane at the Frankfurt, Germany, airport. I finally landed at Cairo International Airport, and it was a bit of a culture shock. I had never been to Egypt, and I had some mental images of what I was expecting, but I wasn't prepared at all for what awaited me. As I wove my way through the massive crowd, smells surrounded me that I had never noticed in an airport before. There were goats and chickens running around the airport. I kept my eye out and finally found what I was looking for: a local Egyptian with a sign that read U.S. EMBASSY. We identified each other, then I went with him out to the Embassy van. The van was armored and had bulletproof glass. Rhode Island was far behind me now.

Driving to the hotel, I noticed how densely populated the poverty-stricken streets were. The air was brown, the ground was brown. Everything was dirty, dusty, and brown. I hadn't slept much on the ten-hour international flights, so when I got into my room I checked in with the squadron and then grabbed a two-hour nap. Next, I went into the control room we had set up. It was nice to see some familiar faces—the Secret Service, the military aide, the White House staff—but everyone was trying to pull together a last-minute plan.

I needed to know exactly when the squadron would arrive, so that I would know how long I had to find hangar space for the aircraft. I found out that we had eight hours, and it wasn't lost on me that Colonel Demars was on the flight as well. Against all odds, I worked with my counterparts and local authorities to secure some hangar space. Once the squadron arrived in a massive C-5 cargo plane, I coordinated to have all the helicopters secured in a nearby hangar. Over the next two days, we had time to rehearse the mission and even ended up with one day of downtime before the President arrived. This was my first time in the Middle East, and I wanted to see as much as I could. The night before, I had asked one of the Secret Service guys what he thought about my doing an early-morning run through the city. He advised me that based on the predominant religion and culture in the area, running around with my PT uniform probably wasn't the most respectful thing to do. I had to agree. Instead, I worked out in the hotel gym, then spent the day meandering through packed alleys, walkways, and shops, marveling at the diverse culture and the colorful wares for sale. The way people dressed, the languages they spoke, the smells of exotic cooking—it was all so new to me, and, as I said, the city was more densely populated than any I had ever visited before. People seemed to live and work and shop shoulder-to-shoulder.

I bought some papyrus art paper for my family and, on a recommendation from a buddy, some Egyptian cotton shirts. Later in the afternoon, I met up with other members of the squadron for a tour we had scheduled at the famous Cairo Museum. I felt like I had wandered into another time as we strolled past the King Tut exhibit and the House of Mummies.

The mission to Egypt was a total success, and once I got the squadron back on their C-5, I had one final day left in Cairo to wrap things up. On the long flight home, I took it all in and imagined the President flying back to the United States on *Air Force One*, and the HMX-1 crew in the back of a C-5 with the white tops and all our equipment. I had just completed a major international mission that honed my rapid-planning skills to an even finer point—and I felt a deep sense of accomplishment.

CHAPTER 4

SEA KINGS AND WHITE HAWKS

None of the incredible experiences I was having at HMX-1 would have been possible if I had not passed all the certifications and levels of training that accompanied my four-year tour. Shortly after flying the CH-53 support helicopter on that first Presidential lift to Detroit, I had to attend the ground school for the VH-3 (Sea King) and VH-60 (White Hawk) helicopters. These are the classic white tops I had daydreamed about for so long.

The ground schools were run right there at Quantico by Sikorsky Aircraft Corporation, and included two weeks of in-depth classroom instruction. Just by virtue of the fact that I had been selected for HMX-1, it was assumed that I was already an experienced aviator. In a typical aviation squadron, new pilots check into their squadrons with about two hundred hours, which is all instructional flight time. At HMX-1, even the newest freshman pilot showed up with at least fifteen hundred flying hours—the minimum requirement. Consequently, the combined flight hours in any HMX-1 cockpit were significantly higher than average, and therefore you always ended up with what we called a "seasoned cockpit."

Next, we entered the pilot-training syllabus, which included about fifty flying hours in each aircraft. These were big-boy rules, not the basics. These highly advanced courses had been systematically designed to build on our experience while teaching us all the nuances of flying a VIP platform. The training was so comprehensive that I probably could have gone through an entire mission, from start-up to shutdown, without even looking at a checklist. As I progressed through each level of training, and instantly applied what I'd learned to real-world, high-profile missions, something else was happening, too: I was falling in love with these machines.

Our primary aircraft was the Sea King, and since it was the platform we utilized the most, it became the icon of the squadron to the public and in the media. The Sikorsky Aircraft Corporation had built our Sea Kings in the 1970s in Stratford, Connecticut. And ever since then, the aircraft have been lovingly sent back to their maker every fifteen hundred flight hours for any modification or upgrade that has been approved for contemporary executive service. The Sea King was originally introduced in the U.S. Navy in 1961 as the Sikorsky SH-3 Sea King. It was the first amphibious helicopter, and when it entered service, it was also the first antisubmarine-warfare helicopter to feature turboshaft engines. At almost fifty-five feet long, almost seventeen feet tall, and with rotors that had a diameter of sixty-two feet, the Sea King's two turboshaft engines could still propel you through the sky at up to 150 miles per hour and at a range of 450 nautical miles. Even in the event of an engine failure, the other engine had enough power to maintain safe flight. The combination of the engines, the power system, and the overall design resulted in a very enduring and reliable platform.

The VIP variant of the Sea King is designated the VH-3, which was later configured for executive transport. The body of the aircraft is aluminum. All the sheet metal for aircraft built in this period is predominantly aluminum because of its strength, light weight, and flexibility. Composites were not yet being widely used at the time. There are countless rivets on an aircraft of this size, as with any aircraft constructed of aluminum sheet metal forming a "skin." On a conventional aircraft, the rivets have worn and become smooth from countless flight hours (friction) and coats of paint (and dirt and grease). Because this aircraft has specialized paint, the rivets stand out uniquely in a marvel of design engineering. Many professional photographs of the Sea King seem to highlight the beautiful linear patterns of the rivets.

The exterior is painted a deep, dark green and covered with a gloss or clear coat that you might find on a classic car. And while the green and white paints do not have a specific name, per se, they have become the hallmarks of the aircraft, and points of pride. The crew chiefs spend countless hours keeping the paint shining to a high gloss. When you approach the helicopter, you can see your reflection. When it is time to "accept" an aircraft coming back from high-level maintenance at Sikorsky, nine times out of ten, my maintenance guys would reject the aircraft the first time around because of the tiniest flaws in the paint. Once the aircraft is finally accepted, the paint scheme is flawless. There is even one particular area of the aircraft—the front port side, where the President approaches and enters—that is so highly scrutinized it has its own inspection criteria. This was also the most photographed area of the helicopter.

The helicopter has a tricycle-landing-gear configuration, with two main mounts amidships, and a dragging tail wheel at the aft station of the aircraft. An American flag and the Presidential Seal plaques were slid into brackets during Presidential lifts. And then UNITED STATES OF AMERICA was emblazoned on both sides. Looking up, you can't help but notice the top portion of the entire aircraft painted in a gleaming white. And above that, five rotor blades, each approximately thirty feet long, drooping gently down toward the ground near their ends.

The only entry into the Sea King is what is called an air stair, much like the air stair on a corporate jet. Once inside, the cockpit is to the immediate left, and the passenger cabin opens up to the right and rear of the aircraft. The interior is in mint condition, fully carpeted in a clean gray color. Even the cockpit is carpeted, which was unheard of thus far in my career. The cockpit windows meet the specifications of any aircraft cockpit glass, as do the cabin windows in the back. The windows in this aircraft have other properties that are classified due to the nature of the mission.

With Wi-Fi, satellite TV, emergency phones, and a slew of other classified communications systems and defense measures, HMX-1's Sea Kings are designed to serve as a flying Oval Office. There are comfy executive seats that could accommodate a dozen guests, and then a special seat for the President himself. The typical smell of oil and grease is nonexistent. Yes, there are always snacks and beverages. The staff knows what the President, his family, and his guests like.

The ride in a white top is much smoother than in most other helicopters, and advanced soundproofing technologies make it easy to hold a conversation in a normal tone of voice. This was another highly unusual feature, and another creature comfort to which I was not accustomed. With regard to the type of business conducted on *Marine One*, there have certainly been numerous affairs of state conducted in that cabin, and secure, classified phone calls about the most critical issues. God forbid there was ever a nuclear strike or counterattack, but whether it's in the Situation Room, the motorcade, *Air Force One*, or *Marine One*, the President will never be separated from his protocols and codes that govern such strategic decisions.

The Sea King flew like a 1976 Cadillac De Ville drove—smooth and true, as if floating on a cushion of air. The aircraft itself can fly normally loaded at 120 knots, but I have flown it much faster when empty. Because of the design and age of this aircraft, the aerodynamic properties are somewhat limited. Fourth-generation aircraft with technologically enhanced rotor blades and composites can fly much faster. Still, even they are hindered by the aerodynamic principles of a rotary wing and antitorque device (tail rotor). It's pure physics. The maximum altitude or "service ceiling" of any helicopter varies, but for the most part they become aerodynamically inefficient at altitudes above 10,000 feet. The rotary-wing design and density of the air have a huge impact on the aircraft's ability to maintain altitudes any higher and still fly efficiently.

The rotary wing of a helicopter when spinning at 100 percent power is extremely fast. It actually turns into a disk, or "rotary wing." The root of the rotor blade (the part closest to the hub of the rotor head) spins the slowest. Out toward the tip, or the very far end of the blade, it spins at close to Mach speed (.88 Mach). It can actually turn so fast that you can "over speed" the rotor system if improperly handled. The physics of a turning rotor are absolutely fascinating, and the tip of a blade achieves greater speed depending on the overall length of the blade.

Marine One is certainly supported by the finest security our nation has to offer (all of which is utterly classified). In terms of maneuverability, the flight characteristics of *Marine One* are equal to those of any aircraft of its type. You can't really mess with aerodynamics. In other words, there is no warp speed or whisper-mode button as fictionalized in the movies. As with any aircraft, it's ultimately the skill of the pilot that will swerve it out of danger. This amazing helicopter was developed more than four decades before I ever set foot in one, but it was by far the most elegant, precise machine I had ever flown.

If the Sea King represents the smooth glide of a Cadillac, then the VH-60 White Hawk flies like the low, tight, and responsive ride of a Ferrari. Sikorsky developed the platform back in the 1970s, and it is now basically a hybrid, executive version of the Army's UH-60 Black Hawk and the Navy's HH-60 Seahawk.

Unlike the Sea King, the White Hawk's pilots enter through carlike doors on each side of the cockpit. The primary entry for passengers is a set of double doors that swing outward with the two VIP seats facing each other as you look into the cabin. Unlike the Sea King, the main cabin in the White Hawk is separated from the cockpit by a wall. The cutting-edge cockpit features digital gauges and numerous classified navigational and communications technologies. The interior is once again plush, with seating and accommodations for up to eleven passengers.

The White Hawk is slightly smaller than the Sea King, making it easily transportable and ideal for overseas missions. The rotor blades can be quickly folded backward over the fuselage. The aircraft can then be loaded into a single cargo plane such as a C-17, including the crew and the entire contingent of support personnel and equipment. Within just a few hours of landing, it can then be totally configured and ready to fly.

White House Hack

The next step was saturation training, which required me to spend six weeks living in a facility near Reagan National Airport, and training on a four-day-on, two-day-off schedule. During this highly classified training, I learned all the intricacies, idiosyncrasies, methodologies, tactics, and principles of transporting the President of the United States.

With saturation training complete, the next rite of passage was to become qualified as a Helicopter Aircraft Commander (HAC) in the VH-3 and the VH-60, otherwise known as "White House HAC" training. This regimented training was tried and true, and planned well in advance, as I was still working and participating on various missions. I completed my White House hack training just before the flight with the Pope. I now had the authority to sign for the aircraft and play a more key role as the primary pilot on a Presidential lift. I was fully qualified to fly as primary pilot for any passenger in the world—except the President himself.

I also had to become qualified as a White House copilot. As was the case in any FAA or aviation certification or evaluation, all the training culminated in a final evaluation flight called a "check ride." Before long, I was designated as a certified Presidential copilot by the Secret Service and the White House. I could now serve as the copilot of an aircraft crew that carried the President, Vice President, or any number of VIP passengers, to include visiting heads of state.

I once read that Igor Sikorsky built his first helicopter at the age of nineteen, using sketches by Leonardo da Vinci. Today, Igor Sikorsky is a legend, his creations proudly transport the President of the United States, and each lift is a testament to Igor's incredible sense of style and engineering. His magnificent machines could defy gravity, and were loyal as a dog if you treated them right. After spending more than a thousand hours in the air flying his Sea Kings and White Hawks, I am forever grateful to Igor. The man was a genius.

Leaving HMX-1: Hail and Farewell

My four years at HMX-1, so rich with excitement and challenge, flew by at the speed of light. A month or so before I left, I received my new orders. My next assignment was Operations Officer at HMH-463, a Marine Heavy Helicopter squadron headquartered at Marine Corps Air Station Kaneohe Bay, Hawaii. I would be flying CH-53s again.

Leaving was bittersweet, but I had been out of the "fleet" for four years, and I knew that this tour could not last forever. In a way, I also couldn't wait to move to Hawaii, to get back into the CH-53 and join the boys in doing what I was trained to do. We were a military family, and we knew the drill. We sold the house and prepared for yet another move.

One of the greatest perks of working at HMX-1 is that whenever someone leaves the White House Military Unit, they get a photo with the President. I showed up at the White House in my Dress Blues for the occasion and was escorted to the Oval Office. Although I had seen the Oval Office with my parents, we had not been permitted to step inside. This time, I was escorted in, and President Clinton greeted me and began making conversation. He asked where I was going next, and I told him about my next duty station in Hawaii. The feeling of standing there with the President for a few short moments, and in that historical room, almost took my breath away. The photographer took our picture, President Clinton shook my hand again and thanked me for my service, and I left.

Walking back out through the corridors of that building, I was lost in thought and grateful for that chapter in my life. I would have to turn in all my equipment, but I kept the patches. I also had the plaque and the photographs. Most important, I had created the most amazing memories and friendships, and nothing could take those away. I cut through the West Wing on my way to the exit, and thought with pride that this would surely be the pinnacle of my career. Little did I know I'd be back someday.

CHAPTER 5

BECOMING THE COMMANDER OF HMX-1

1996–2006: The Road Back to HMX-1

I had been out of the "fleet" for four years, and I was pumped to get back into the CH-53 and join the boys in doing what I had originally been trained to do: fly helicopters and plan helicopter operations, in preparation for combat. When I reported for duty at HMH-463, there was an instant sense of familiarity with being back in a "normal" assignment, but it also took me a while to reacclimate to the new organizational structure and pace.

The leadership positions of any flying squadron are held by field grade officers, and the two primary and most coveted positions are Aircraft Maintenance Officer (AMO) and Operations Officer (OPSO). These two positions are mutually supportive of each other, and a squadron will fail if it does not have competent people and sound synergies in place in both of these integral leadership positions. Finally, the squadron leader also becomes one of the lead pilots. When I left the fleet I had been a Captain. Now I was a Major, which is a field grade officer. Not only that, but I was a Weapons and Tactics Instructor course (WTI) graduate and held every flying designation allowed. Since I was also current in the CH-53, during my three years there I spent time in the AMO role, and as the OPSO, and as the Executive Officer (XO).

My next "assignment" was Command and Staff College back at Quantico. The Marine Corps puts a great deal of value into Professional Military Education (PME). Command and Staff College was just that—a career-level school for field grade officers who have the potential for command. In fact, without this level of schooling, you will not even be considered for command. The aggressive curriculum lasted an entire year and included many different facets such as operational planning, strategic thinking, political science, an intense writing course, a series of leadership discussions, and weekly guest speakers from various specialty fields. The student body itself was comprised mostly of Marines, but also included at least twenty international students, people from each of the other military services and a number of civilian agencies. I was promoted to Lieutenant Colonel in 2000, right around the time I completed Command and Staff College.

Once again, it was time to move back to Hawaii, since I was then assigned to the United States Pacific Command (PACOM) as the Command and Control Systems Chief. Basically, I was in a supervisory position, running the Command and Control Systems Branch. When 9/11 happened, I became one of two Crisis Action Team briefers, which gave me a lot of face time with PACOM leadership. One of those senior leaders was Admiral Tom Fargo, and based on my performance in PACOM and my reputation as an effective WHLO back at HMX-1, I was eventually recruited to serve directly on the Admiral's personal staff. Specifically, I was his Deputy Executive Assistant for a year, which was an extremely high-level staff position. Militarily speaking, Admiral Fargo was responsible for 53 percent of the planet, which included forty-three nations (not all of them friendly). He reported directly to the Secretary of Defense (Donald Rumsfeld at the time), who in turn reported directly to the President (George W. Bush).

The Admiral was also loved and respected, which made you want to work your butt off for him and never give him cause to be disappointed. Although fifteen-hour days were extremely common, this was one of the most rewarding positions of my career. Not only did I work for a man I respected deeply, but just being in that circle of strategic planning and decision making provided me with an education I could not have obtained elsewhere.

While still serving in this position, I was selected to command the famous HMH-362 "Ugly Angels" squadron. It was one of three CH-53D squadrons that provided combat helicopter support for the infantry units in the Pacific Theater (all the ground units within Marine Forces Pacific). The Ugly Angels is a very storied squadron, and the name had been garnered from years of service in Vietnam. Over the years, the squadron had transitioned into different platforms and relocated to several different bases. The overall size of the unit had also decreased for many reasons. By the time I took command, the Ugly Angels had been relocated to Hawaii (its final home) with roughly 150 Marines.

There was an immense and dare I say perverse pride in being an Ugly Angel. We walked with a certain swagger, and we played very hard. But the reputation was well deserved since we accomplished every task with conviction and vigor, and with consistently superior results. As if that wasn't enough, our call sign to air traffic controllers was "Ugly," and I don't think I need to comment on how much fun was had with that. I led the unit from 2003 until 2004.

My increasingly broader leadership roles were very demanding, and I was busier than ever. When I wasn't working, I was still training for and competing in local triathlons. I was also enjoying the island culture with family and friends. In my mind, Hawaii was the only place I had ever been that could top California's lifestyle. By this time, Ray Jr. and Delia had finished their schooling. Delia was now in law school,

and Ray Jr. had joined the Marines and completed OCS, officially chang-
ing the number of Marine Officers in the L'Heureux family tree from
one to two.

They say that the stars must really be aligned for you to get selected
for the position of HMX-1 Commander and Presidential Pilot. It's a
very rare and unique assignment, and you need specific "boxes" to be
checked. Among other things, you must have served in HMX-1 previously, and you must be a Colonel (or selected for promotion). Finally,
you can't lead HMX-1 unless you have successfully commanded an operational squadron.

Next to Infantry Officers, pilots are the second-largest group in
the Marine Corps. Typically, there are more pilots eligible for command than there are squadrons to go around. The environment becomes
highly competitive, and most Marine pilots don't ever get an operational command. They may not get a command at all, and they might
spend their careers in various staff positions, like the one I held at PA-
COM. They could also become a monitor. Every Marine Officer has a
monitor assigned to him or her, and this individual's job is to monitor
your career progression, provide guidance, and help get you into the
right schools and assignments.

Even if you did meet all these criteria, it still wouldn't help to de-
mystify the very idea of becoming the President's pilot. You don't even
apply for the job; you get hand-selected for it by the top leadership in
the Marine Corps. For all these reasons, it would have been preposter-
ous for me to plan on going back to HMX-1. The odds just weren't in
my favor. I already had enough experiences and memories to last a lifetime, and how lucky could one guy be? Since 1996, I had been slowly
moving in exactly the right direction, and when I was promoted to
Colonel in 2005, I had apparently checked the final box. Before long, I
began to hear some rumors from colleagues that I was actually being
considered for command of HMX-1. My experiences in the squadron

came back to me full force, and still stood out as some of the best times of my life.

HMX-1 was not part of my daily life anymore, but it was the favorite chapter in my book of memories, which included a lot of memorable chapters: Flying the Pope; Walleyball with President Bush on Camp David; My years as a WHLO; The D-day trip with President Clinton. Now, the son of the first President I had reported to was President! To say I was intrigued is a gross understatement. I kept reminding myself that others were being considered as well, and I tried to stay stoic about the whole thing and keep my excitement at bay, even to my closest friends.

But it *was* actually possible. I had just completed an operational command, and now I was a Colonel. Secretly, I wished despite all logic that I would get the opportunity of a lifetime.

The Sikorsky Fellowship

The Marine Corps is a culture of continual learning and development, and after my Command assignment, it was time for yet another level of training. Many Colonels go to War College, which is a graduate-level military education run internally by the respective military branches. These schools are considered career milestones and can mark a transition into more executive-level roles. But there are also a number of fellowships that are designed to balance military experience with a year in academia and industry.

At the time, there were fellowships at Rand, Tufts, Wharton, the Harvard School of Government, the Kennedy School, and one called the Secretary of Defense Corporate Fellowship. The overarching goal of this last program was the open exchange of ideas—for Marine Officers to help civilian executives with leadership skills while gaining a better sense of corporate and business operations.

Each year, different companies can participate in the fellowship, and the year I was selected, they were FedEx, Johnson & Johnson, Raytheon, Insitu Group, Symbol Technologies, Georgia Power, Sun Microsystems, and United Technologies. Out of the eight students selected for the Secretary of Defense fellowship, I was the only Marine Officer. There were also three Air Force Colonels, two Army Colonels, and two Navy Captains. I listed my top three choices, with United Technologies being number one. Based on my unique experience, the administration of the fellowship thought that Sikorsky (a subsidiary of United Technologies, and the company that built most of the Marine Corps' helicopters) would be the best fit.

The week before I left for the fellowship, I was sitting at home on leave, and I received the news that changed the course of my life.

My home phone rang. It was an old buddy, Justin "Scourge" Wisdom, whom I'd known ever since my first assignment back in California. Incidentally, we were in the same unit and he was there when Steve and I first saw President Reagan land in *Marine One*. Now Scourge was serving as the Commanding Officer of HMT-301, the training squadron for the CH-53D.

After some small talk, he simply said, "Congratulations, bubba . . . you are the new Commanding Officer of HMX-1."

I started peppering him with questions like, "So the list came out? How do you know?"

"I have the list right here in front of me, Frenchy. You got the job! I'm so happy for you, man."

A full decade after I took that farewell picture with President Clinton in the Oval Office, a board of Marine Generals had selected *me* to be the twenty-second Commanding Officer of HMX-1. I hardly remember the rest of the conversation with Scourge, because in my mind, I was flying a VH-3 again—hovering over the White House lawn at dusk or looking down at Central Park in New York from 200 feet. Most important, I felt absolutely blessed that I would have the opportunity to lead Marines once more. After we hung up, I tried to remain calm as I told my family about the call, then started calling everyone else I could think of to share the news.

Each call started with something like, "You're not going to believe this . . ."

It took me a few days even to process the information and accept the reality of my next assignment. At one of the first board meetings to kick off the fellowship at Sikorsky, we all went around the table and introduced ourselves. There were chief executive officers, vice presidents, and other stakeholders present. When it was my turn, I introduced myself and explained my background. I remained humble and expressed how happy I was to be there, but it quickly became clear to me that they all knew I was the heir apparent for HMX-1. This was an important mission for Sikorsky, and they were intimately involved in HMX-1's culture. After all, you probably couldn't get better advertising or product endorsement than having the President of the United States fly in your company's aircraft. The eight of us started out with a full month in Washington. We spent time in the Pentagon and on Capitol Hill, talking to various politicians and leaders and getting to know more about the types of projects and initiatives we'd be participating in. As I settled into the fellowship, I tried to learn all that I could. At one point, each company also hosted the other fellowship participants for about a week.

The whole experience gave me unfettered access to the leadership of all the participating companies. I gained insights that I never would have had by attending War College, and I was grateful for the collaborative experiences. All the while, seemingly whenever I had free time, I was researching HMX-1 and current events. By understanding current events, I could glean some information and make assumptions about the types of missions HMX-1 was coordinating for the President. And the types of missions I would soon be expected to lead.

We had been at war in Iraq for a couple of years. Hurricane Katrina hit New Orleans in August 2005. The political scene was intense. Since President Bush had already begun his second term, I knew that once again I would be part of the transition between two Presidents.

The feeling reminded me of times in my life when I had my eye on a new car, for example, and all of a sudden I saw the specific model and color I wanted everywhere. Since I was aware of it internally, I was noticing it externally. Now I had HMX-1 on the brain. Every time I watched news coverage of the flood, or of the White House, there was *Marine One*, dutifully transporting the President. But as I watched the news and geared up for my next assignment, I didn't just see the sleek green-and-white helicopter that most people probably noticed; I could actually feel the stick in my hand, feel the responsiveness of the aircraft when I pushed the pedals, and hear the engines starting up. I could still imagine *Air Force One* barreling toward me and then watching President Bush or President Clinton waving and walking down the steps.

I had learned and grown so much since the last time I had flown those amazing birds. Other things had not changed, like the fact that HMX-1 was still the best job I had ever held. Now it was almost time to begin the most exciting and challenging role of my life and career. I was ready, but I must admit that I could already sense the daunting responsibility that was about to be placed on my shoulders.

Returning to HMX-1

I finished the fellowship and reported back to HMX-1 in the summer of 2006. Whenever a new Commander comes on board, he spends around nine months shadowing the outgoing Commander, learning the ropes again, and getting recertified as a Presidential Pilot. My predecessor was Colonel Andrew "Junior" O'Donnell (Drew). We were friends and had served at HMX-1 together during our first tour. I felt very

lucky to be receiving the squadron from him. As I observed the operational rhythm of the squadron and began the task of reacquainting
myself with squadron life, I asked a million questions and he patiently
answered them all. When I flew the Sea King for the first time in over
a decade, it was like meeting an old friend.

Of course, I was very familiar with HMX-1 operations, but things
had changed on so many levels. For one thing, I began to gain insight
into aspects of HMX-1 that I hadn't even considered the first time I
was there. It had simply been above my level back then. For example, I
knew that HMX-1 included military police, but in my first tour I had
not realized that we actually had the largest military-police company
in the entire Marine Corps. I had around one hundred MPs, including
a K-9 unit. From an organizational standpoint, the entire culture felt
different than it had under President Clinton. I could tell that this squadron had known only President Bush, and that they had been through a
lot. As a result of September 11, the ensuing war in Iraq, Hurricane Katrina, and countless other things, the country had changed. HMX-1 culture had changed along with it. Surprisingly, I didn't hear a lot of stories
about the Bushes at Camp David, but I did hear people mention the
ranch in Crawford, Texas.

Not only was I shadowing the outgoing commander at all his meetings, and getting recertified to fly the white tops, but I was also just observing and feeling out the organization. Before I even met President
Bush or formally took command, I had a great opportunity to do that.
The President had plans to return to New Orleans and Mississippi for
the one-year anniversary of Hurricane Katrina.

I was in the Sikorsky fellowship when Katrina hit, and I saw all the
media and news coverage just like everyone else. Since I had already
been slated as the next CO, to a certain degree I was able to follow
HMX-1 in terms of logistics and timeline. By calling key contacts, I

tried to follow the mission from afar. Now I was going down to see what the city looked like a year later. I was very intrigued because, aside from driving through the area and layovers at the airport, I had never actually spent time in New Orleans. Also I had flown only a couple of times since leaving the Ugly Angels, and I was excited to get back into the cockpit.

The trip leader was Major Garret Hoffman, and we were going to fly four aircraft from D.C. to Louisiana (two VH-60s and two CH-53s). I was going to fly one of the CH-53s in the lift package. I'm sure it was an unusual experience for Major Hoffman and the other pilots to have a full bird Colonel, and their next CO, flying a supporting aircraft. My goal was simply to learn, observe, and see the squadron in action.

We left early on an August morning and arrived around dinnertime. The flight took us through various types of airspace and over several states. As we came into the northern part of New Orleans over Lake Pontchartrain, I could still see the remnants of a long bridge that had been swept away. Soon, we were flying right over the city, making wide-sweeping turns to set up for the landing to the south, and I could tell that something had gone horribly wrong there. In some areas it looked like the storm had hit the day before: devastation, trash, abandoned neighborhoods, and countless blue tarps on still-unrepaired roofs.

I looked down and thought, *Holy crap, this place looks like a war zone.*

We finally bedded down at a Naval Air Station in Belle Chasse, which is a few miles south of New Orleans proper. Before we descended for landing, I saw in the distance the seemingly endless marshes. From studying my map, I knew that this vast geographical area was where the Mississippi River transforms and washes out into the marshes that dominate the southern tip of Louisiana.

We then drove rental cars to our hotel, just blocks from the French Quarter. The hotel was fine, and I couldn't tell whether it had been affected by the storm. We had an early morning, but we did go out for dinner, then explored the area just a bit. Really, besides a few spots that seemed abandoned and washed out, the entire French Quarter felt pretty much like I had expected it to—a party atmosphere full of music and fun-loving people.

One of my favorite rituals is to take a run around a city in the early morning, especially if I've never been there before. I almost always get the bird's-eye view of a place, but my morning runs give me a chance to get the lay of the land in another way. So, a few hours before work began the next morning, I went for a run around downtown New Orleans. I ran a few blocks to the river, then turned left and followed it for a couple of miles. I made my way in toward the French Quarter, and passed Jackson Square and the Saint Louis Cathedral. As I ran through the humid and historic streets, I couldn't help but admire the stunning architecture. Deep in the heart of the French Quarter there was little evidence of a hurricane or flood.

I may have been too distracted by the sights and sounds. As I approached Bourbon Street and looked left and right, I saw a car slowing down at the intersection. I also saw that I had the green light and right-of-way on my side. I slowed down but kept running and began to cross the street. I then noticed on my near left that the car wasn't slowing down after all. I actually had to jump onto the hood so that the bumper didn't hit me. I rolled off the hood and hit the ground. The car didn't stop. I stood up slowly and did a self-inspection. Nothing was broken, and I was okay, but I did have road rash on both arms and legs.

A man nearby had been cleaning the street when I got hit, and he had seen the whole thing. He asked if I was okay. I looked down again. My scrapes were red and bleeding a bit, but not too bad. "Yeah, I'm fine, thanks." I said, then decided to finish my run. "Welcome to New Orleans."

A few hours later, we were doing rehearsals, coordinating with the

WHLOs, and just getting everything prepped for the two days of lifts. It was refreshing for me to see the amount of professionalism demonstrated by everyone involved. The squadron had integrated some new technology since my first tour, but overall the rhythm and process were the same. On the first day, we flew the President to the Ninth Ward, one of the areas most affected by the flooding. As we landed in a field, I saw President Bush from a distance, and I wondered what it was like for Major Hoffman. We also flew him to visit a school that had been rebuilt since the flooding. Out there on the edges of New Orleans, some progress could certainly be seen, but then again there was still a great deal of trash and seemingly abandoned neighborhoods.

The press was there all along, of course, capturing everything. The next day, we picked up Haley Barbour, the Governor of Mississippi, and flew over the state's coastline. New Orleans had taken all the headlines, because of the flooding and state-leadership issues. Many people don't realize that the Gulf Coast of Mississippi took a direct hit. Although this area was not as large as New Orleans, it did appear that much more work had been completed there. I flew over the large concrete slabs that had once held casinos and resort hotels. There were construction cranes everywhere, and the sense that progress was being made.

We got the President back to *Air Force One*, and from my vantage point in the cockpit of my CH-53, not far behind *Marine One*, I saw him climb the airplane's stairwell and step inside. For the first of many times, I then watched him take off in the huge jet, until it was only a tiny airplane fading into the distance.

Meeting George W. Bush

During this period, I also took several trips back to Camp David. I had not been there since the days of Bush 41 and Clinton, and I soon found out why I wasn't hearing much talk about Camp David. Apparently, the current Camp Commander had created a culture of separation. He encouraged all military personnel to stay "out of sight, out of mind" whenever the President and his family were in residence at the camp. I was surprised and a bit disappointed to hear this, because I remembered how much it meant to us when we interacted with President Bush 41.

On this particular visit, I had just landed with another pilot, Major Jim Toth. It was around 5:00 P.M., and we were traveling down a paved path on our way to the lodging area when Jim abruptly pulled the golf cart off the path and into the woods.

"What are you doing, Jim?"

"Sir, the President is right in front of our cabin," he said, as if I should understand his actions based on this statement. I didn't.

"So, why did we pull into the woods?"

"Oh, we were told not to bother the President when he's on Camp."

"Why would we bother him? He'll think we don't like him. Pull on up, Jim."

He looked at me cautiously, as if to say, *You're the boss,* but he did as I'd asked.

As we pulled up, President Bush, wearing jeans and a windbreaker jacket, was trying to coerce into the golf cart the black Scottish terrier we had all seen on the White House lawn. "Come on, Barney, come on," he said.

We parked right beside his golf cart, and I respectfully said, "Good evening, sir. Do you need any help?" I was smiling politely because we both knew he didn't really need my help with the little dog.

The President looked at us and said, "How are you doing tonight, fellas? No, I think I've got it under control." Then he laughed and said, "Can't you see he's ferocious?"

We shared in the joke and wished him a great night. He returned the gesture and didn't seem the least bit bothered by our presence. I had a feeling that I would spend many weekends at Camp David, and that night I made another mental note: the culture at Camp David would be changed.

A Day in the Life

In June 2007, we held a formal change-of-command ceremony out on the flight line, and Colonel O'Donnell said his goodbyes. When it was my turn to speak, I mentioned just how privileged I felt, and thanked Drew for all his help and guidance in preparing me for this huge responsibility.

The clock had officially started ticking, and I began settling in to my tour as Commander. One of the first things I did was move into my new office. Located in the heart of HMX-1 HQ, it was a small room with wood-paneled walls. Photographs of former HMX-1 Commanders and the last few U.S. Presidents lined the walls.

My desk sat on one side, with a small wooden table and two chairs positioned in front. On my desk was my computer, along with secure and nonsecure telephones. It was bigger, but—in an odd way—it wasn't much different from the desk on which I had built model airplanes when I was a boy. Beside those I placed some photos of my family, and there were framed posters of several aircraft on the wall behind my desk. On the other side of my desk, in customary fashion, were two flags in a metal stand that allowed the long wooden poles to crisscross. One was the American flag, and the other was the official Marine Corps Standard, or the squadron colors. It was just another office, but now it was my office. On the table across from my desk stood a replica of a Night Hawk helicopter, forever frozen at an angle in midflight. It could have hung from my bedroom ceiling when I was a boy.

In so many ways, I was still the boy who couldn't wait to get home and open the box of his new model airplane, but here I was, the head of HMX-1. It was both empowering and daunting to be in charge of such a large and talented workforce. I had learned a lot as Commander of the Ugly Angels, but this was a new kind of challenge. I now had a great number of aircraft and four entirely different models under my command. There was the VH-3 Sea King, the VH-60 White Hawk, the CH-43, and the CH-53E.

I also had eight hundred "employees," including Marines, Sailors, and "civilian Marines." Among them, I had what were considered some of the top helicopter pilots in the Marine Corps and hundreds of support personnel specializing in maintenance, communications, security, and safety, to name a few. The ranks of my diverse workforce ranged from Lance Corporals (E3) to Lieutenant Colonels (O5), and there were various ages and educational and cultural backgrounds represented. My immediate staff was comprised of the normal complement of field grade officers, an extremely seasoned and competent group.

My perspective had changed, too. I was no longer a young boy or the recruit at boot camp or that young Captain or Major serving as a copilot. I was now going to be the Presidential Helicopter Pilot, with ultimate responsibility for the success or failure of all of HMX-1's complex operations. All of HMX-1's diverse training, operational testing, and executive support missions fell under my scope of responsibility, and I was accountable to three different chains of command. We provided testing and evaluation of helicopter systems for use across the Marine Corps and helicopter support for various Department of Defense training missions.

Most important of all, though, was the Executive Support mission: I would be flying the President, his family, his staff, and a multitude of other dignitaries and government officials all over the world. Most aviation organizations have a specific Area of Responsibility (AOR), but because of the Executive Support mission, our AOR spanned the entire planet.

Quite often, after a twenty-five-year career, the Commander of an aviation squadron does exactly that—command; he or she does not necessarily fly very much. But HMX-1 was different, since the Commander of HMX-1 had the billet description of "Presidential Helicopter Pilot." I was considered one of the old men by that point, but I still got to fly almost daily, just like the young pilots. And although I orchestrated HMX-1's global missions through my talented staff, at the end of the day, the organization's fifty years of operational perfection were mine to mar.

My days and weeks were filled with a combination of complex planning, flying, and leading young and old Marines, always instilling growth and introducing a human element to the job as well. I also strove to mentor my staff to new heights of professionalism by fostering an environment of continual learning and development. The ready room was our professional and social nucleus, as in any squadron. It was a modest room with rows of chairs, and a large podium and counter up front where the Operations Duty Officer sat. Behind that was the "grease board," which was again so prevalent in any aviation ready room. Back in the day, this would have been a clear Plexiglas surface that we wrote on with grease pencils. Modern technology has since transformed it into a large flat-screen monitor with a digital version of the flight schedule, but we still called it a grease board.

Each morning, we held an All Officer's Meeting (AOM) in the ready room to get everyone on the same page. On any given day, there were twenty to forty pilots and copilots in the room, along with other administrative and support personnel to include our civilian contractors and technical representatives. It was not as simple as a landing on the White House lawn or on a school yard in New Jersey. The safety and security of the President and our pilots were always the top priorities. There are countless other decisions, preplanning, and actions that had to take place for everything to run seamlessly. Still, anything could change at any moment, so my staff had to be flexible and dynamic in the face of those possibilities.

Assimilating my higher-level guidance from my boss and the White House Military Office, I synchronized HMX-1's activities to be as efficient as possible. Under my guidance, the Operations Department developed a daily and monthly flight schedule to ensure that each trip, lift, and mission had the right talent and mix of capabilities to meet the particular mission set.

When there were multiple missions taking place at once, I needed a few other pilots to act on my behalf. I hand-selected four command pilots based on maturity and capacity to make decisions when things were not going as planned. The command pilots had to undergo some additional training to be qualified to fly *Marine One*, and then I did a final check ride with each one. One of those pilots was Major Jennifer Grieves, who was the first female *Marine One* pilot in history. When she joined the squadron in 2005, she became only the second female to do so. In May 2008, I selected her as one of my command pilots. On July 16, 2009, Jennifer led the first all-female *Marine One* crew when they picked up President Obama on the White House lawn.

We were Marines, and we knew how to follow orders. That's how the chain of command was supposed to work. In order to carry out my orders, and to provide direction to the workforce, I made daily decisions internal to HMX-1 operations. I also sometimes made decisions that directly affected the President himself. I had an enormous responsibility when I had the President in the air. For those few minutes or hours, his life was in my hands, quite literally. That responsibility alone could be quite daunting. The Secret Service was integral to mission planning and security, but at some point they had to relinquish a level of control until I landed the Boss safely at his destination.

As a helicopter pilot, I was very cognizant of the impacts of weather on aviation operations. Safety is always a critical planning factor, but in combat training you were not dealing with VIPs, so you learned to deal with highly adverse weather situations. Being the Commander of HMX-1 took weather considerations to an entirely new level, as I was not going to put the President in the air if there was any kind of weather risk. I now had access to the country's most advanced meteorological reports and analyses, which I used to make critical decisions on whether or not to fly. These kinds of decisions were some of the most agonizing because we ran a zero-fail mission. My decisions had to be precise and every possible course of action and effect had to be taken into account. Plus, let's face it, nobody wants to say no to the President, and nobody wants the embarrassment (and possible disciplinary action) of making the wrong call.

I was mandated by White House standard operations procedures to make a weather call at a certain point in time, which was but one small decision point in the larger, complex, and nonstop scheduling and coordination effort. For example, thunderstorms often roll across the property in Crawford, Texas. There were times that the Secret Service asked me for the weather call, and procedure made the decision more frustrating. My boss was all about following strict protocol, and I agreed. I knew how a deviation from policy or process could cause a domino effect of issues at multiple levels. It wasn't worth the risk. Still, I remember standing there in Texas looking up at the sky and talking to the Secret Service guys.

I told them I had been watching the radar and that I knew we'd be clear in two hours, when the President was scheduled to leave the ranch. But at that exact moment in time, when they needed a decision so that they could coordinate (or not) a motorcade and get local law enforcement involved in blocking off roads, I simply couldn't approve the lift. On the other hand, I could use the informaiton at hand to approve the lift, but if the weather didn't clear up as predicted, then the Secret Service would have to scramble to put together the motorcade, and I would be the squeaky wheel in an otherwise well-oiled machine. Worst of all would have been if the weather was actually bad and I made the decision to fly the President, and put him in danger. Luckily, this never happened during my tenure. It was always better to be safe than sorry, period.

During one of the many weekends at Camp David, I was standing on the porch of my cabin Sunday morning, eyeing the weather. It didn't look good. Camp David was socked in with thick fog. I could fly in the rain as long as I had visibility. I knew that appearances could be misleading, so my copilot called the Camp David weather office for the official meteorological reports. I quickly realized that if things went my way, I would have a safe window of opportunity to get the First Family off the mountain and back to the White House. But if things went another way, I would not have visibility, and would not be able to fly.

Safety was my most important deciding factor, but I was also aware of the domino effect my decision could have. If I decided that we could not fly, then the Secret Service, Camp David personnel, and local law enforcement would all have to work together to plan and secure the route for the President's motorcade. This would not be so uncommon, but then again it was an inconvenience for the local communities, and took a lot more time and energy than just flying him home in his helicopter. In my opinion, a day like that was probably one of the reasons *Marine One* became such a preferred method of travel.

I called the military aide and told him about my concerns.

"They're just about to head off to church. Should I tell them we have to go?" he asked.

"No, not yet. I think the weather is going to break in about an hour, but then there is another band of nasty weather coming our way. As soon as the weather breaks, I will be sitting on the landing zone and I'll call you with a five-minute warning."

I packed up my stuff, drove over to the hangar, and positioned the aircraft at the landing zone. I kept in close contact with the weather folks, and then it was time. I had maybe twenty minutes to get him off the mountain and out of the weather. It was going to be a bumpy ride, perhaps, but I was willing to accept that and knew that I could fly safely.

I called the military aide and said, "If the President wants to fly, it's now or never."

He then told the President, "Colonel L'Heureux says if we want to get off this mountain by helicopter, we have to leave now."

The President was a pilot himself, and he understood. The vast majority of the flying we did with him on board was done by what is called "visual flight rules" or VFR. This basically means that you're flying in clear weather, and you can see where you're going, so you manually control the aircraft. When the weather doesn't allow for enough visibility, you fly under "instrument flight rules" or IFR. This means that the air traffic control (ATC) folks guide you through certain airspace on a predetermined flight path. And since you really can't see where you're going, you rely on the ATC's deeper visibility of the entire airspace, and their ability to guide you using the technology and instrumentation on board. It's not autopilot. We're still flying the helicopter, but navigation and other things are determined by the ATC.

My least favorite thing about flying the President in IFR was that if something happened to the aircraft, or there was any type of emergency at all, I would not have the capability to land. I wouldn't be able to see the ground below me. Instead, I would have to declare an emergency in flight, which would initiate another ATC protocol for those types of situations. Finally, in an IFR scenario, the whole lift package didn't fly in our normal formation, using "eyes on" to orchestrate our aerial maneuvers. Instead, each aircraft was being vectored and guided to our destination by the ATC system.

As I checked the helicopter and positioned it on the landing zone, I coordinated with ATC for IFR support and airspace priority. I felt

Flight student, freshman year, Nathaniel Hawthorne College, Antrim, New Hampshire, 1979.

On stage, third from right, top row: Winging class, Whiting Field, Florida, May 1986.

2nd Lieutenant L'Heureux, flight school, 1985.

Instructor Ensign Walt Rossi, flight school, Pensacola, Florida.

Left to right: Captain Rich Hall, 1st Lieutenant L'Heureux, 1st Lieutenant Alex Gierber, 1st Lieutenant Steve Paquette, Republic of Korea, 1987.

The dreaded and feared "helo-dunker," Pensacola, Florida.

My father and me at Ray Jr.'s commencement.

Commanding Officer, HMH 363, Lieutenant Colonel "Willy" Willard, 1988.

Commissioning my son at Virginia Military Institute commencement, May 2004.

With my father and son.

Emotional tribute, outgoing change of command, HMH 362 Ugly Angels, 2004.

Presenting the President with his one-of-a-kind Marine One mountain biking helmet, 2009.

After an especially bloody ride, 2008.

Taking a break while building the biking trail on Prairie Chapel Ranch in Crawford, Texas, 2008.

President Bush exits the aircraft.

Meeting Pope John Paul II, World Youth Day, Denver, Colorado, 1994.

Pope John Paul II exiting Marine One, New York City, 1996.

Marine One crew during President Bush's visit to Windsor Castle, 2008.

President Obama bids farewell to former President Bush, Inauguration Day, January 2009.

Marine One lifting off from the South Lawn.

pretty good about the conditions. I had spoken to the White House, and I knew the weather was clear there. Within a matter of minutes, the First Family approached the helicopter, their golf cart dripping rain off the sides of the plastic roof. Then it was all umbrellas and walking lightly through the wet grass and up the stairs. My crew chief stood beside the stairs, as usual, and saluted as our passengers boarded. They quickly shook out umbrellas, removed their raincoats, and took their seats. Then the President stepped into the cockpit, slapped me on the shoulder, and said, "Let's get out of here, Frenchman!"

I lifted off seemingly right into a massive cloud. I could see the size and shape of the cloud bank in my mind. In close coordination with ATC, I followed the flight path and eventually rose above the clouds. Once they set me on the final approach to Ronald Reagan Washington National Airport, I canceled IFR and proceeded visually. Within forty minutes, we landed safely on the South Lawn, where the sky was sunny and clear. I had made the right call.

In 2007, I had the unlikely opportunity to serve with Bayou and Spanky again. As part of HMX-1's Operational Testing and Evaluation role in the Marine Corps, we were fielding a new Presidential helicopter. I decided to assign a team of five officers to work with the White House, Lockheed Martin, and other agencies to coordinate the project. I knew firsthand how uncommon it was for anyone to come back to HMX-1, unless he came back as Commander.

Then again, anything was possible, and I knew that Bayou and Spanky had the kind of institutional knowledge and technical expertise we needed. I thought about this issue long and hard, and even discussed it with Willie. Eventually I approached my boss, the Marine Corps Deputy Commandant for Aviation, and proposed that we reassign Bayou and Spanky back to HMX-1 as part of this special team. I knew they were both nearing retirement and looking for assignments back in

Virginia, so it would be a win-win for everyone. My boss approved the decision, and Bayou and Spanky joined me back on our old stomping grounds. It would be the last assignment in both of their careers, and they loved it.

My First Ride with Peloton One

The Marine Corps is like many other organizations in at least one way: word gets around quickly. By the time the new guy comes on board, especially the new boss, everyone knows everything about him. Now I was the new boss, and I learned later that I was known as the forty-something *Marine One* pilot who loved competing and who could apparently outrun most people in the squadron.

As the new Presidential Pilot, I stayed connected to the President, his staff, and his operations schedule through his five military aides (one each for the Army, Air Force, Navy, Marines, and Coast Guard). I quickly began to form strong relationships with each of the aides.

The first time I flew President Bush to Camp David, I was waiting on the South Lawn of the White House with the engines running. He would be coming out the doors at any moment. The Air Force military aide was standing in the cabin of *Marine One*, chatting with me and my copilot. I asked him about these rumors that the boss was into mountain biking.

"The President used to run a lot. But a couple of years ago his knees got pretty bad and the doctor told him to lay off the running. Now it seems like he brings his bike wherever he goes," the aide said. "In fact, we'll be biking forty-five minutes after we land today. We call it bike ops."

"Wow, really? I ride triathlon-style bikes when I compete, but I've never tried mountain biking," I said.

"Well, the Boss is in really great shape. He goes all out," he said.

I watched the President approach the aircraft and salute my crew chief, who was standing outside near the steps. The military aide moved to his seat. I listened and watched for the crew chief to board the aircraft, then secure the steps. That was my cue. I called for clearance over the radio, and lifted off.

It was a sunny afternoon with low winds, and I was pleased that the flight was so smooth. When we landed at Camp David, the President came up to the cockpit, slapped me on the shoulder, and said, "Thanks a lot, fellas." Then he climbed into his golf cart and drove to his cabin.

I was still taking care of post-flight procedures—going through my checklists and making sure the aircraft was tucked away nicely in the hangar—when I saw a group of mountain bikers moving quickly through the trees. *Goes all out . . .* I thought.

A couple of hours later, I was settled into my cabin, and I received a call from the Air Force aide. He must have spoken to the President about our conversation on the South Lawn. He said, "Hey, the Boss invited you to join us for bike ops tomorrow morning."

I said, "Awesome. Thanks!"

"Okay, be in front of the President's cabin at eleven A.M.," he said.

Some of the rumors about me were true. I was passionate about physical fitness, and I felt that I was in pretty decent shape. Marines are supposed to be tough, and the Marine Corps obviously promotes fitness, but senior officers are sometimes seen as slower or less fit than the younger folks. As a seasoned Colonel, I took pride in leading by example. I fell asleep imagining a nice ride through the back country on Camp David, maybe even getting in some good cardio before hitting the gym later in the day.

The next morning I was up early and ready to go. Someone had already put a couple of "mountain bikes" in front of the guest cottages for the pilots to get around camp, each with a helmet hanging off it. I didn't know it yet, but there is a big difference between real mountain bikes and the knockoffs some people call mountain bikes. These loaners had very basic components, they were pretty heavy, and they had little or no suspension—not exactly what you want when flying down mountain trails at high rates of speed. Innocently, I just picked one at random.

I wore my Marine physical-training uniform, which consists of running shoes, a pair of small, nylon running shorts Marines refer to as "silkies," and a green T-shirt. I hopped on my bike and pedaled over to the President's cabin. By that point in my career, I had met dozens of famous people, interacted with Presidents and their families and staffs, and even gone hiking with Pope John Paul II. I was not one to get "starstruck." But the thought of going mountain biking with a President was totally unexpected and, I had to admit, just really cool.

When I pulled up to the cabin, I exchanged good-mornings with the dozen or so people already waiting for the President to come out. There were a couple of Secret Service guys, several other people I knew who worked on camp, and some of the President's friends from back in Texas. It was a stunningly sunny June day, and everyone was cheerful and friendly.

I like to think that I am an intuitive guy, and I realized pretty quickly that I stood out from the rest of the group. No one else had a loaner bike like mine. Theirs seemed bigger, newer. They were all geared up with specialized biking equipment, and there I was in my running gear. They had on special shoes that clipped into their pedals. They all had on spandex shorts, gloves, and CamelBak hydration systems. It was a bit like showing up to a Ferrari convention in a Volkswagen bus. Everyone was kind enough to resist blatant mockery, but I guessed by their shared looks that I seemed pretty ridiculous showing up to a serious ride in just my silkies.

Pretty soon, President Bush came out of the cabin with a bounce in his step, all geared up and full of energy. He smiled and said, "Good morning, fellas. Great day for a ride!" He was wearing full mountain-biking gear, including a mouthpiece, helmet, a blue shirt made of a kind of Gore-Tex mesh specifically designed for biking, shorts, and sunglasses. His iPod earplugs were hanging down over his shoulder. He just looked like one of the guys.

He noticed me and said, "Colonel?"

"Yes, sir?"

"You must be Frenchy."

Obviously, the military aide had told him my call sign. I said, "Yes, sir, I am."

"Welcome. Glad to have you on the ride. Have you done this before?"

"No, sir, I have not."

It was only a nanosecond, only a beat, but I saw the knowing smile in his eyes that would make a lot more sense later. Then he nonchalantly started describing the plans for the morning.

"Okay, first we're going to warm up a bit around camp, just to get our heart rates going. We'll do some speed trials on a technical single track and then hit some unimproved trails on the other side of the mountain too."

He was using a lot of biking jargon, and I basically had no idea what he was talking about. I just kept nodding my head and saying, "Yes, sir. Roger that, sir."

Finally, he put in his mouth guard and started leading us toward the trails. I still couldn't believe I was mountain biking with the President. Within twenty minutes, that feeling of exuberance was gone and I realized I was in way over my head.

I was already sweating, and my silky running shorts had turned into an evil saw between my thighs. The "technical single track" that the President had so calmly explained was actually a challenging course of rocks, logs, bumps, and hills. There is no nice way to say it: my bike was a piece of shit.

I soon learned why everyone else's feet were clipped into their pedals.

When they approached a bump or log, they simply pulled the front tire up, bent their legs, and let the bike's suspension system do its magic. But seemingly every time I went over an obstacle, my feet came off the pedals or the chain came off. Then the opposite pedal would spin around and hit me in the shin.

My pedals were made of metal, with sharp spikes for traction, and before long I was sweating and bleeding profusely from my legs. At times, I had to get off the bike and carry it over logs or other obstacles. Nobody stopped. Nobody slowed down. The President didn't even look back. It was almost noon, and it was growing hotter by the minute. Unlike the other riders, I had come unprepared, and had no CamelBak or water bottle.

My body could get me through a lot, but this was a new experience. A new skill set. Muscle memory that simply did not exist. As my frustration and fatigue grew, I thought to myself, *Okay, this really sucks. In fact, it really hurts.*

My pride also kicked in. I had been invited to ride with the President. I was a United States Marine, for God's sake, and I couldn't keep up on a bike? I was not going to be the guy who dropped out. I silently swore that I would die on that trail before I let that happen.

I kept pushing on, trying to keep up, and cursing my bike. At one point I hit a log while going downhill, and I flew headfirst over the handlebars and into the brush. Someone said, "You okay, Colonel?" as he flew by.

I didn't want any help. I didn't want the attention, so I said, "I'm fine, fine." I stood up, checked for broken bones, and climbed back onto that sorry excuse for a bike. I checked my watch and saw that it had been almost two hours of nonstop hard-core mountain biking.

I was bloody, hot, dehydrated, and pissed off at being so unprepared. I was not having fun. I was in survival mode. There is a saying in the military that some physical challenges are 5 percent body and 95 percent heart. I was clearly working on the 95 percent by this point, relying on my stamina to overcome my lack of skill. Somehow I was keeping up, but just barely.

Eventually, we came to a flat area at the bottom of a long downhill ride. I was painfully aware that Camp David rested on the top of a mountain, so the more we rode downhill, the farther we would have to climb back up.

There was a moment when my front tire was parallel with the President's back tire. He looked over his left shoulder at me and asked, "Well, Frenchman, what do you think?"

Of course, I wasn't going to give him an inch. I was not going to admit that I was being dogged. I said, "So far, so good, sir."

He said, "Okay good, good. We have to climb this mountain, so we're gonna hit this little single track and take it straight up. It's going to work your quads a little bit."

I looked up. I couldn't see the top of the hill. If a President had ever understated something, this had to be it. *Work your quads a little bit, huh?*

I said, "Sounds good, sir."

Although they all had the right gear and precious water, they seemed to be reaching their physical limits by this point. I was thinking that the agony of climbing this hill would be a huge improvement to the last couple of hours. If I could just keep my feet on the pedals, and the chain didn't come off, I could make it. This ride would end.

I switched into low gear, leaned forward, put my head down, and started pumping. Everyone was breathing hard, and my heart was beating in my ears. The next thing I knew, I started passing some of the other riders. A couple of Secret Service guys just got off their bikes and started walking them up the massive hill.

When we got maybe three-quarters of the way up the hill, it was only the President and I. I just kept pedaling from moment to moment, trying to keep up with him.

He looked back at me. He was breathing hard and pumping those pedals as he asked, "Frenchman, are you sweating yet?"

This was not a good time for me to talk. I wasn't just sweating, I was bleeding and battered. I had been irritated for hours. Now I was mad at the hill and mad at the stupid bike and mad at myself. I was beyond physical exhaustion, in a lot of pain, dehydrated, and a little delirious.

Of course, I didn't think about all that at the time. Instead, I just said, "Fuck yeah, I'm sweating!" I don't know if the President heard my exact words, because he always rode with an iPod. I saw him chuckle just a bit with that familiar raising of his shoulders, though. We both kept pressing onward and upward. Even in my state, I realized instantly what I had just said. I thought, *Oh my god. Oh my god. I just dropped the F-bomb on the President. I'm done. I'm toast.* I was mad at myself once again for the lapse in judgment.

The President and I finally reached the top of the hill, and we both were heaving to catch our breath. He looked at me while he took a long drink of what must have been delicious water. He noticed that I didn't have any and offered me some of his.

"Frenchman! You did okay," he said. We stood there for a while next to our bikes while everyone else was catching up. He didn't say anything about my comment, so I assumed that either he hadn't heard me or he didn't care.

Within a few minutes, we were pedaling on the paved road that led back to the cabins. All of the mountain bike rides began and ended in front of the President's cabin. I was elated that the ride was over. I had made it. As we milled around a bit, talking about the ride and taking off our gear, the President offered to take a photo with me.

In biking jargon, a peloton is simply a group of riders. Apparently, the President's mountain biking group came to be known as Peloton One. If it was your first ride, you got a pair of biking socks that said PELOTON ONE on them and took a photo with the President.

We posed for a quick picture near the trees in front of his cabin.

The President looked at me and said, "Frenchman, you did really well for having a piece-of-shit bike."

I laughed and said, "Yes, sir."

"You're going to need a better bike," he said. Then he looked over at his aide and added, "Let's make sure that next time the Frenchman has a better bike."

He looked back at me. "All right, Frenchman, you need to get some shoes and gear, and the guys will work on getting you a better bike."

I couldn't believe he was already talking about the next ride. Maybe he hadn't heard me after all.

After a few comments to the other riders in the group, he said, "Okay, fellas, good ride. I'll see you later," and he went back into his cabin.

Now that the excitement was over, the pain really hit me. I was happy and amazed that I'd just had the opportunity to ride bikes with the President, but I was also assessing the damage.

I had gashes up and down both legs. I had whip marks across my arms from branches. I had blisters on my hands. My inner thighs were beyond raw. I skipped the gym that weekend.

When I got back to my cabin and into the shower, everything stung. But as always, I couldn't wait to call everyone and share this latest adventure. Before going to bed, I spent more than an hour telling the story a couple of times. The next morning, my entire body was stiff, and I couldn't lift my legs without pain. For about the next week, back at Quantico, I borrowed my wife's car to drive to work because it hurt to climb up into my Jeep. I smelled like rash cream and Bengay for days.

I would learn later that President Bush loved his Marines, and he also loved to test people on their first ride with Peloton One. I also found out that this had been the first time he had invited his pilot on a ride, and that most rides were not nearly as long.

I never dared to ask him if he had heard my F-bomb as we climbed that final hill. The military aide told me that when the President heard his new pilot had a reputation for being physically fit, his expressed intent that morning was to dog me. I'd say he succeeded. All I knew was that there was more to this man than met the eye, and he would never call me "Frenchy" again. I had officially become "the Frenchman."

CHAPTER 6

GETTING TO KNOW THE PRESIDENT

Crawford, Texas

When I tell people some of the stories from my time as a Presidential Pilot, the conversation often turns to politics. I don't mind discussing politics with my friends, but many people are surprised when I tell them that politics had absolutely nothing to do with my job. The President's politics were completely irrelevant to HMX-1, aside from the fact that his very job was political, and that job defined our schedule. Our mission was to provide executive-lift support for the President and his staff, wherever they wanted to go, and regardless of why.

First and foremost, being a Presidential Pilot was my job, and I was accountable to the White House Military Office for performing in that role. Aside from that, I would say it was much more personal than political. This is because, for some reason, the President gave me the opportunity to join him as part of Peloton One, his mountain biking club. Mountain biking seemed to be his favorite pastime, his favorite form of exercise, and I guessed it was probably therapeutic as well.

Obviously, the life of the President is fast paced and very demanding. And even though my role as HMX-1 Commander was also demanding, my primary role was to accompany and support the President wherever he went, as much as possible and as needed. Since the President used Camp David as the Presidential retreat it was meant to be, I found myself using it in the same way: as a refuge of relative quiet amid a chaotic job and schedule. Those weekends spent at camp are some of my most memorable.

The same thing applied to the ranch in Crawford, Texas. The First Family lived in the White House for most of the year, but they spent many weekends and each August on their ranch in Crawford. That was home, and the President was even more relaxed and in his element there. Just like Camp David, I became a regular visitor to the ranch, and rode bikes there with the President many times.

Sometimes I had to pass—I mean, I was working when I was there; but whenever I could, I was all in for the rides. I was still competing in triathlons, and this mountain biking also gave me a chance to work out. Riding with the President was never just a relaxing pedal through the back country. He was really good, and this was hard-charging, advanced riding. Just as with HMX-1 itself, there was no room for incompetence in Peloton One. If you couldn't keep up, you probably wouldn't be invited back.

As time went on, I always shared the mountain biking stories with my staff and everyone at HMX-1, and included them as much as possible. The President was also very friendly and generous about it, always taking pictures with any new riders. Even as Marines in the largest aviation squadron in the Corps, we still had a certain amount of downtime. This was not a bad way to spend some of it. I didn't let it go to my head, but my workforce was well aware that their boss was getting to ride with President Bush. I'm pretty sure they thought this was cool. I know I did.

Every single move the President made, including every bike ride, was carefully tracked by the Secret Service and on certain radio frequencies. The details of who went on the rides were also transparent, and my name was mentioned more and more as my life synced with the President's schedule. Even my leadership was aware of these activities. I was at a meeting in the White House one afternoon, and my boss, a two-star Admiral, looked at me with a grin and said, "How is the President, Frenchman," using the nickname the President had given me.

The first time I actually flew the Boss to Crawford, I had visited the ranch only briefly while still transitioning into my role as Commander. I didn't know much about the ranch at all, except that the family called it home. We flew down a lift package to a civilian aviation facility in Waco, Texas, a couple of days before the President arrived. The squadron members always stayed in a hotel in Waco. We also had a small facility on the ranch itself, with a small hangar, a double-wide trailer, and a helicopter-landing pad. Marines assigned to Crawford worked in shifts. There was always going to be some downtime, and we had an arrangement with Baylor University to use their gym, but I'm also pretty sure some of my Marines took full advantage of the local dating possibilities. . . .

One day *Air Force One* landed at the base, and I was waiting in *Marine One*. The President and the First Lady climbed aboard, and I flew them to the small helipad on the ranch. I then flew over the countryside back to Waco and put the helicopter away for the night. The military aide called later to tell me that I had been invited to ride bikes on the ranch the following morning.

The drive from Waco to Crawford is about forty-five minutes and takes you through rural Texas farmland. With a mountain bike in the back of my rental truck, I showed my credentials at the main gate. I then parked near the HMX-1 trailer and rode my bike through several other Secret Service checkpoints that led to the compound where the President actually resides.

The mountain biking bug finally bit me, as I'm sure the President knew it would. I was pumped to see what kinds of trails he had on the ranch. I thought it couldn't be that bad. It was flat, right? The last time I was this wrong, I was misjudging the Marine drill sergeants at Parris Island. There is a flagpole near his home, and this is where I was told to link up. When I rode up, a few people were already there, including some Secret Service guys, some local friends from the area, and the military aide. Two of the ranch hands were also riding this morning. I was introduced, and found out later that the President called them "the Dirken boys." They were good riders.

Everyone was geared up, stretching out, and it was already turning out to be a hot August day. My CamelBak would serve me well. The President emerged from his house right on time, in a great mood as always. He greeted his friends, and said, "Hey, meet the Frenchman!" The President was ready to ride, and in a matter of minutes he had put on his gloves, his helmet, and his iPod, and he led the pack. We spent about fifteen to twenty minutes warming up on a flat area of the ranch, and I again thought this was going to be a lot easier than Camp David.

Little did I know that there was a large canyon on the ranch. If you were to look at the ranch from a satellite view, it would appear as if someone had taken a huge cleaver and dug out a five- or six-mile stretch of land. We dropped down into this canyon, and the riding suddenly became much more technical and challenging. Everyone was working hard to keep up with the President as he flew over the washboard trails, maneuvering his bike over hills and rocks.

After some time, we stopped at what looked like a trailhead. Everyone drank some water. I then joined the President, the Dirken boys, and the Secret Service guys as we left the bikes in place and started hiking on a crude and unimproved trail. I noticed some wooden markers nearby, and some engineering flags. The President explained to me that he had invited members of the International Mountain Biking Association to ride on the ranch, and that they had helped him map out this two-mile trail. It was clear that the President intended to build the trail eventually, but right then it didn't look much like a trail. It was just a beautiful, overgrown canyon.

Over the next couple of years, the President strove to turn his vision into reality. There were people working on the trail when he wasn't in Texas, but when he was there, he did not shy away from the work himself. And believe me, it was hard work. There was a trail marked out, but for it to take shape, countless trees had to be cut down, boulders dug out, ground smoothed out.

I still had not forgotten how Marines avoided the President on Camp David when I returned as Commander. I also had not forgotten how much we appreciated interacting with President Bush 41 and President Clinton. I saw the trail as a potential way to make some positive changes to the culture I had inherited at HMX-1. I knew I was usually going to be in Waco when the President was at the ranch, so after one of my first rides there, I asked, "Do you need any help, sir? I might be able to round up a few volunteers."

He said, "Well, we can definitely use all the help we can get." He then looked right at me and said, "Frenchman, make sure they are volunteers only," putting emphasis on the word *volunteers.*

"Roger that, sir." I knew what he meant. I was the Commander, but he did not want me to order my Marines to come out and help on their personal time. I would never have done such a thing.

If I had gone back to Waco and told my Gunny, *Hey, I need some volunteers to go and do backbreaking, heavy-lifting work in the field in the hot sun,* you would have seen Marines scurrying into the woodwork. This was an unusual situation, so instead I said, "Gunny, the Boss needs some help with some trail-building on the ranch and he's open to volunteers." I then looked at him in the serious way the President had looked at me, because this was not a joke. "This needs to be one hundred percent volunteer only. All I can tell you is that they will work their asses off, and if they haven't already, they will probably get to meet the President. I've volunteered to help out tomorrow, and I'll take up to ten volunteers."

Once word got out, it seemed as if everyone in Waco that weekend wanted to help. I could have easily taken more, but I stuck with ten Marines. I then told my Gunny that the uniform would be jeans and work clothes. The next morning, I met my volunteers in the parking lot and gave them a quick briefing. I thanked them for volunteering, and explained that they might meet some high-level leadership, and just to address anyone they were introduced to as "sir" or "ma'am."

We drove to the ranch in rental cars and then climbed into the backs of pickup trucks and moved to the trailhead. The President was already there waiting, along with his National Security Advisor, some White House staff members, and the Dirkin brothers. The President was wearing jeans, a T-shirt, boots, and a baseball cap.

In his usual animated fashion, he smiled and said, "Holy cow! Here's the Marines. Hi, fellas, how are you?" He shook their hands and introduced everyone. He then addressed me directly: "Frenchman. These Marines are all volunteers, right?"

"Absolutely, sir," I said, as my Marines nodded in assent.

"Well then, thanks for coming out. Let's get to work." We all grabbed tools out of a nearby pickup and followed the President and his guests down the trail. I could hear chainsaws and sledgehammers up ahead.

The work crew developed a certain rhythm, almost like the way railroad workers would have laid tracks back in the day. There was a team out in front doing clearing, cutting through trees with chainsaws, digging up rocks with shovels or breaking them up with sledgehammers. The next team in line worked on flattening and leveling the ground with hoes and rakes. Yet another team or two would come behind to fill in any areas needed to ensure that the trail was wide enough, and just to make final touches. At times, progress was incredibly slow, and we would all get stuck on one spot for hours at a time. The President always led the way on the front team, and almost always preferred to do so with a chainsaw.

Eventually, the sun began to set, so we all walked off the trail, dusty and tired. We had worked hard, and the President thanked us as we loaded all the tools into the bed of his pickup. We took a group photo near the pickups. He was so kind and appreciative to the kids, and they got to see a side of him that they never would have seen otherwise. I could tell that my Marines were thrilled to be hanging out with the President, and I could only imagine how much fun they would have sharing the photo with their families and friends. The President was grinning from ear to ear when he drove away in his truck. I'm quite sure this had been a new experience for him, too.

I helped out many more times, and before long, trail building got rolled up into my open invitation to ride bikes. If I was in the area, I would coordinate through the military aide and bring volunteers if possible. Word spread quickly around HMX-1, and many Marines seemed to appreciate the opportunity to do something very different on their downtime. I also made it clear that the President did not expect our help, but that he certainly appreciated it. All who volunteered confirmed this, sharing their own personal experiences from the ranch. Considering Major Jim Toth's reaction to seeing President Bush on Camp David, we had already come a long way in creating a more inclusive culture between the President and the squadron that supported him.

President Bush often caused those around him to laugh out loud. During one of our bike rides not long after that day, my CamelBak had pulled my shirt up, and the President noticed a small tattoo I have on my lower back. He asked, "Frenchman, what is that on your back?" I quoted Jimmy Buffet and said, "Sir, that's a permanent reminder of a temporary feeling." I further explained that I'd gotten the tattoo during the early years of my ongoing infatuation with the Hawaiian surf and triathlon cultures. From that point on, when I brought some of my Marines on a bike ride or to help with the trail, after introducing them to the President, he would say something like "Has your Colonel showed you the tattoo on his ass?"

I'll never forget a time at the ranch when his humor was unintentional. On this particular day I had brought perhaps a dozen of my Marines, all of whom had volunteered as usual. In this extremely sweaty and tough trail work, the President was leading the front team. He was working the chainsaw and overseeing a section of the trail that had just been cleared of trees and rocks. As was very common in the course of a typical "work day," he yelled over the sounds of our laboring, "I need the hoes. Get my hoes up here."

As chance would have it, two of my female Marines had volunteered that day, and yes, they were working the hoes. Hearing the President's voice, they quickly ran up to the front of the crew and stopped short when they reached him. There was an awkward silence as the President, my two Marines, and everyone else realized what he had just said. After a brief pause, the whole group busted out laughing. It was such a human moment, and so endearing to watch the look on the President's face when he realized what he had said. No one was offended. Nothing needed to be said or explained, because we all knew that the comment was completely unintentional. He just needed the hoes up there to get the trail cleared!

On a couple of occasions, I actually spent a few minutes alone with the President, or as alone as one can get with the Secret Service close by. I was invited to ride on the ranch one day, and went through all the checkpoints, making my way to the flagpole. I was expecting to see a

group of people, as usual, but I was the only one there besides two Secret Service guys.

The President came out in a jovial mood, all geared up, and said,
"Okay, Frenchman, are you ready?"

"Yes, sir!'

As we took off, the Secret Service guys kept up with us, but at a
distance. It was clear that they weren't necessarily along for the thrill of
riding this day—they were just trying to keep up with the Boss and his
helicopter pilot. We stopped every so often to drink water and just take
in the view. There wasn't much conversation, as we were both out of
breath and both wearing iPods.

At one point, I watched his back tire slip in the dirt and he almost
crashed. It reminded me of an icy ride on Camp David one winter morning. The President's tires had slipped on the ice, and I watched him slam
into the ground, all tangled up in his bike. The Secret Service was immediately at his side, but he just stood up, shook it off, and finished the
ride.

He didn't crash this time, but the moment and the memory once
again threw me into nostalgia. As I pedaled up a hill, trying to keep
up, I thought to myself, *The whole world is going about its business, and
someone may be thinking, "What is the President of the United States doing
right now?" I can tell you what he's doing—he's riding bikes on his ranch
with a bucket-head Marine Colonel!*

We made another stop and the military aide caught up to us in a
four-wheeler. He handed the President a cold bottle of Gatorade. The
President proceeded to chug about half of it down, then handed me the
bottle and said, "Frenchman, you want some Gatorade?"

I thanked him, took a few gulps, and handed it back. He didn't
think anything of it at the time, and neither did I. For a moment, we
weren't President and Colonel—we were just two dudes out on a ride.

●　　●　　●

On another day, months later, the trail was nearing completion. I had volunteered to help out, and was busy breaking up a boulder. I happened to be separated from the rest of the group when I noticed the President walking toward me on the trail.

As he approached, I said, "Hey, Boss, what's going on?"

He said, "Just surveying our work. Hey, take a walk with me, will you?"

I put down the sledgehammer and followed him up the trail. I could hear voices and the sounds of the work crew around a bend. We walked about fifty feet farther up the trail. On one particular turn, one of two things needed to happen. We could cut down some large trees, but that would mean extensive excavation and backfill work. Or the trail could go underneath a rocky ledge, which would mean a lot of digging to ensure there was enough clearance.

We just stood there examining our options and discussing the best ways to complete that segment of the trail. Eric Draper was the White House photographer at the time, and, like the characters from the movie *Men in Black*, he seemed to show up everywhere. He came walking down the trail and, upon seeing us standing there, snapped a candid shot. To this day, it's one of my favorite photos of all time. By the time President Bush left office, we were riding the completed trail. He did an interview with Sean Hannity after his presidency, and they were walking on the mountain biking trail we helped to build.

Perhaps the most vivid memory that demonstrates our mutual respect and friendship happened back at Camp David. The Peloton was killing the trails one day, completely in the groove. Toward the end of the ride, we were going down a steep single track, and my handlebars clipped a branch. I had wiped out before, so I knew what to expect. I hit the front brake too hard and went head over heels down this hill.

I did a somersault in the air, twisting to avoid landing on my back. I came down hard on my side and slid a few feet in rock and gravel. I immediately checked for broken bones, and when I found none, I got up and checked out my bike. It was fine. I had a good case of road rash, with several abrasions on my right arm, leg, and thigh bleeding freely. I hopped back on my bike and kept riding.

When we stopped, everyone was cooling down, discussing the ride, and the President was only a few feet away. He saw the blood dripping from my arm and leg and said, "Holy shit, Frenchman! Are you bleeding again?"

I said that it was nothing, then he said, "Damn, Frenchman, that looks bad, but it's also the best wound we've ever had at camp. We've got to get a picture."

A few moments later, the Camp David photographer came over. President Bush bent over to get a closer look at my leg, and said something to make me laugh. The photographer snapped the picture right at that moment. As I turned my head to say something to one of the other riders, I felt something and looked down.

The President had poured some of his drinking water on my leg and was cleaning my wound up with his bare hand. I was quite taken aback, because where I came from, only a dear friend would do something like that without hesitation. This man was my Commander in Chief, and the President of the United States, and he was worried about me? This lasted for a few seconds, until a Camp David nurse walked over to assess the damage.

When we departed Camp David that Sunday afternoon, the President handed me a copy of the photo. Normally, he would sign photos with something like "Ride on."

This time, he quoted something I had said jokingly to him on a previous ride. The handwriting on the photo said, "Frenchman, if you're not bleeding, you're not riding."

In California with the Terminator

I supported the President on a trip to California in January 2008 for a fund-raiser and a meeting with state leadership. There would be multiple lifts over the course of two days, as we were stopping at various locations in Orange County.

On one of these days, California's governor, Arnold Schwarzenegger, would fly with us from Torrance to Brentwood for the fund-raiser. During preparation for this trip, I realized that the President and I had another thing in common: we liked to have a little fun.

For the past decade or so, it had become standard practice to pack our aircraft up into a large cargo plane and fly them to our destination. In the past, it was more common to fly the lift package across the country. Many of my pilots had never done this. In order to ensure that my Marines still maintained those skill sets, and to provide them with a new challenge, I decided that we would actually fly across the country to California with a full complement of five helicopters (including two white tops).

The basic route of flight was from northern Virginia to Barksdale Air Force Base in Louisiana, on to Tucson, Arizona, and then into California. We conformed to FAA rules near any cities, but over the rural areas we flew at 200 feet, which is a very interesting way to see the country. I'm sure this was the first time the people in those towns saw white tops flying over their land.

Since it was January, the weather got pretty rough a few times as we traveled through some major ice storms in Louisiana and Texas. We were forced to land in Texas and spend the night there until the weather broke. Ice actually cracked one of the windshields, so we had to plan for repairs. All along, I was closely watching the clock and calculating whether we could make it to California in time. I even called back to my Operations Department and had them coordinate a backup lift package just in case. Finally, we pushed through and made it to

Tucson, Arizona and then on to California just a couple of days before the event.

It had been an adventurous trip for me and my copilots, and more than once I questioned whether I had made the right call to fly all the way there. The President did not realize the unforeseen challenges we had overcome to get *Marine One* in place, and when he landed in *Air Force One*, we were right there waiting as usual.

Once the event began, and Governor Schwarzenegger climbed on board *Marine One*, he was nice enough to come up into the cockpit and say hello. As I turned around to shake the governor's hand, President Bush's face popped up over one of the governor's massive shoulders with a delighted smile, and said, "Look, Frenchman, it's the Terminator!" The governor just laughed it off. He probably heard that joke a lot, but I'm willing to bet that he had never heard it from his President.

The White House

I was settling in to the high-intensity job of leading HMX-1. I was getting to know my staff, fostering strong relationships with stakeholders in the Secret Service, the White House, and numerous other agencies. I had flown the President on a number of missions. In a very unexpected manner, I had been given an opportunity to show the President my character, and to see him outside the cockpit and on the trail.

I was having the time of my life, and the White House began to take on a whole new level of familiarity. On any given morning, while people commuted into D.C., I drove into Anacostia before sunrise because I had to pick up the President at the White House. Usually I took the helicopter out to burn off a bit of fuel and perform a final systems check. This was probably one of my favorite times of the day, especially in the winter. As I walked out to the flight line in the predawn darkness with my hot mug of coffee, and the aircraft was already warmed up for me, the air was so crisp. I would take off smoothly and start heading up the Potomac. And then there would be a moment when the sun became visible on the horizon. I would make a buttonhook turn to the right, take us up to about 1000 feet, and then do a 180-degree turn. This positioned me at the top of Sixteenth Street, which ends at the front door of the White House. The Potomac looked like a ribbon of light when the sun hit the water.

Now I would fly directly toward the White House as the city woke up below me. Everything looked so vivid as I sat in my warm cockpit with the knowledge that I and my crew were certainly the only people flying in that airspace. I had my office, and I had my home, but at work, the cockpit was my home. I loved the feel of the cushions of the pilot seat, the resistance of the pedals. I monitored the way all systems worked together under my touch, and reveled once again as this great machine obediently followed my commands.

What had been a few lights quickly became a flowing river of red brake lights on I-95. That was their morning commute, and this was mine. All was right in the world somehow during those surreal early-morning flights. Favorite place to work? Check!

After the test ride, I would fly back to the base, grab another cup of coffee, and change into my lift uniform. By the time I came back to pick up the President, the city had risen. At least a few people usually stood outside the White House grounds, waving and taking pictures as I passed by. Once I entered the grounds, there was often another group waiting near the landing zone, this time made up of the media. I was confident in my ability to fly the President safely, but it was a strange feeling for this old CH-53 pilot to have so many eyes and cameras always pointed at my helicopter.

If something were to go wrong, it would be on the national news in a matter of minutes. It was time to focus. Put aside the crazy fact that the President was about to board, and that you might be able to watch your takeoff on the news that night. The President boarded, and it was time to fly him out of there and link up with the rest of the helicopters in the lift package. I may choose to be in front of the other aircraft, in the middle, or in the back. Only we would know which one carried the President. It was always a good feeling to pick him up and execute another successful mission.

I lost count of how many times I landed him on the South Lawn after a long day. Usually this meant that he landed at Andrews Air Force base at night, so I would pre-position *Marine One* an hour before *Air Force One* was set to land.

I knew exactly when that was, but it never got old seeing and hearing the massive plane land and then scream toward me. In the light, I could see the classic blue-and-white paint. Under cover of darkness, the plane's bulk was lined with running lights, and I could see the profiles of Colonel Mark Tillman and his copilot up in the illuminated cockpit. The President then climbed down the steps and walked over to his helicopter, his air taxi. I would then make a short flight back to the White House to bring him home.

Americans seem to have a certain curiosity about the White House, and—before I was Commander of HMX-1—I was one of them. This had been the formal home of every American President since Thomas Jefferson. As HMX-1 Commander, I was an integral part of the decision-making process in the White House Military Office for everything that pertained to helicopter aviation support for the White House. To accomplish this, I became part of a very small percentage of people who get inside access to the White House.

My White House boss was the Director of the White House Military Office, and his office was located in the East Wing. The East Wing is pretty much reserved for all the Protocol folks, the First Lady's offices, and the White House Military Office. My boss required all his subordinate Commanders to come in for a weekly meeting, which was usually held in a conference room in the White House basement. Attending these weekly meetings would be my counterparts in the White House Military Office: the Commander of Camp David, the Commander of the Presidential Aircraft Group, the Commander of the White House Communications Agency, and the Commander of the White House Mess.

On occasion, I was also invited to the White House for formal and social events, such as when someone left the White House staff or the Secret Service. Whether I was there for a meeting or an event like this, I had the right credentials to gain almost unfettered access. Because of my unique role in the President's schedule, I also knew most of the senior Secret Service personnel who oversaw White House security.

I arrived early for meetings, making my way through security, then walking the entire length of the White House to the West Wing, and the old Executive Office Building. There is a cafeteria there, and I typically stopped by for a cup of coffee. Next, I walked through the halls again until I reached the East Wing, and my boss's office. It never got old and I never took it for granted.

Inside, I always felt a certain giddiness that came from being in the most powerful office building on the planet, and being allowed to walk within the storied walls of so much American history. I always remembered taking my parents on the White House tour, and taking the photo with President Clinton in the Oval Office.

On several levels, my second tour in HMX-1 often created a sense of coming full circle. I had gone from young pilot to more seasoned pilot. From Presidential copilot to Presidential Pilot. From freshman to Commander. By 2008, Ray Jr. had been deployed to Iraq twice, during some heavy fighting in Fallujah, and was now assigned to Parris Island as part of the training organization for new recruits.

In a very "full circle" experience, he asked me if I could promote him to Captain. As a CO, the opportunity and privilege to promote Marines to their next rank occurs on the first of each month. It is a highlight for any CO to shake a Marine's hand and say "atta boy" or "atta girl" in front of the entire unit in formation. I always enjoyed participating in these time-honored milestones, and I was thrilled to be able to promote my son. The idea of promoting one's son in front of his peers and leadership not only evokes pride in the traditional Marine Corps sense, but it brings up a deep sense of parental pride. We made the drive down to Parris Island and promoted him in a short ceremony.

As I stood in front of Ray in the position of attention, eyeball to eyeball, and while the promotion order was being read, a sense of emotion came over me that almost dropped me to my knees. There I was, some twenty-eight years after his birth, looking at my mirror image. Same uniform, same name tape, same blood, same profession. Here was my son, walking in my footsteps, but that's where the similarities ended, in a sense.

I was also looking into the eyes of a young Marine who had already seen so much in his short career. You see, my son volunteered during this nation's time of need, willing to serve during a very tenuous time in our history. This was his generation's war, and they will be the new "greatest generation." My son had entered the very exclusive club of the less than 1 percent of the country's population who serve . . . and serve he did. Ray served two tours in Iraq and one in Afghanistan, and saw friends and Marines he served with die in combat.

In my almost thirty years of service, I never once had to bear witness to a shot fired in anger, but my son had been in harm's way right out of the chute. So, in that seemingly endless moment as I stared into his eyes—through the lens of pride, angst, admiration, and love—I also knew that I was staring into the eyes of a Marine Corps Officer who had earned the right to wear the rank of Captain. There are no words to adequately convey the amount of pride that I had at that very moment, and that I still carry with me to this day.

While we were there, we also took the opportunity to look around a bit. There were certainly new structures and buildings after all those years, but so much of it looked hauntingly the same. It was nostalgic to be standing there, especially when Ray Jr. shared funny and crazy stories with me about the drill instructors and the recruits. He said, "Dad, we actually have a new group coming in tomorrow. Do you want to watch?"

I said that I would love to, and I knew that these kinds of visits from other officers were allowed. Then again, I didn't want to cause any trouble with his chain of command. He got permission and I agreed to just watch and stay out of the way. The next morning, I showed up early and watched as hundreds of recruits from all over the country came out of the barracks and began to assemble for first formation. They all stood at attention on the same yellow footprints in front of the same recruit barracks where I had nervously stood one spring day back in 1980.

I silently looked at this young Marine Officer and reveled at the fact that he was my son. Not only that, but he was a Captain and a Platoon Commander at the very same recruit depot where I had begun my career. I was now at the end of my career, and he was at the beginning of his. Yet, he had already been part of a young man's war, and had seen so very much during his time in the Marine Corps. When I snapped back from nostalgia to the present moment, it struck me again just how far I had come.

Wounded Warriors

As a Marine and career military man, I had always been fascinated with the man who was President, especially the way he took up his role of Commander in Chief. Now I had a front-row seat. Years before I became his pilot, I watched President Bush talk to the first responders in New York City after 9/11. I watched him address the nation each year in the State of the Union address. I knew that the war in Iraq was a hot political issue that had polarized the nation.

I had many friends serving in Operations Iraqi Freedom and Enduring Freedom, many of them from the Red Lions and Ugly Angels. In 2008, I took the President to visit some of the wounded warriors. Every other trip he took was a highly orchestrated event in terms of logistics, security, and all the other necessary coordination. There was always press involved, tight security, and very clear start and end times.

Taking the President to visit wounded warriors in military hospitals was different from anything I had done up to that point. For instance, no press was invited, and the President wasn't his usual jovial self. He was much more somber. Also, there was no specific time of departure on this type of trip. It simply ended when he was done visiting with injured military personnel and their families.

The first trip was to a military hospital in Bethesda, Maryland. The trip lasted about four hours, and the President visited with more than a dozen injured service members. He presented them with Purple Hearts, thanked them for their service, and spoke with their families. While he was inside, I waited near the aircraft with the other pilots. Here was the President, pinning Purple Hearts on these injured kids and talking to parents. Although we weren't currently serving in a combat-operations role, we were part of the larger U.S. military machine. We knew it could be any of us in there, and we spoke proudly about the fact that the Commander in Chief was in there visiting our brothers and sisters in arms.

I finally saw the President's limousine making its way back to the helicopter, and I was expecting a very solemn President climbing the stairs, shaking his head, exhaling heavily, just taking his seat and riding back home. To my absolute amazement, when the limousine stopped just beside *Marine One*, the President climbed out with a huge smile on his face. He bounded up the aircraft stairs, ran into the cockpit, smacked me on the shoulder, and said, "Frenchman, it's a good day to be a Marine!"

I did not dare ask the President how he felt about all of it, but I had my own ideas. I heard firsthand accounts about some of the visits. I knew that he had sincerely asked the injured service members, "Is there anything I can do for you?" Many of them had replied, "Yes, sir. Get me back to my unit!"

Even though the country was against the war efforts in the Middle East and the mainstream media would not let up, I believe the President found strength and inspiration in the very people who were fighting in the wars he had sent them into. I took him on many more trips to visit wounded warriors, most of them to Walter Reed Medical Center.

On another visit, the White House press was allowed to go along. I remember seeing the footage on the news, but I had a different perspective than most. I had dropped him off that day and seen his mood. I had been there when he came out. I figured it was as close to being in the room as one could get without being in the Secret Service. I couldn't help but wonder what it must have been like for him to walk in there and face the reality of those horrific injuries, seeing the great loss and anger in the parents' eyes.

From what I could see, he never let the experiences affect him in a negative way. He actually seemed inspired after the visits, as if he was fueled by their sacrifice, commitment, and professionalism. I could only imagine that he dealt with it in his own private space, with his own family and loved ones.

I had interacted with President Bush 41 and President Clinton a few times during my first tour. When I became President George W. Bush's pilot, I expected the same type of interaction. I couldn't claim to understand exactly why it had happened, but for some reason, I was the first pilot the President had invited on the trails. And after that first ride with Peloton One, it almost seemed that I was expected to participate in the rides.

I wasn't going to ask him, *Mr. President, why do I get to ride bikes with you?* I just assumed that since I could keep up, and since my job required me to be wherever he was anyway, he decided to invite me. Regardless of why he did it, I appreciated the opportunities and the memories. Through the media, one gets a certain sense of the President, which is of course colored by any number of personal and political beliefs. I saw the President through that perspective just like anyone else, watching him address the nation and speak on TV.

I also knew firsthand where he was going, and why, and got to witness his overall demeanor as he climbed on and off *Marine One.*

Even so, I didn't get to sit around and have coffee and discuss world politics with the President. We didn't interact on that kind of level. I was his pilot. He was my boss. There was a certain protocol and professionalism, a line in the sand that I would never have crossed. Then again, within the context of our respective roles, we spent a significant amount of time together either in the air or on the trail. In countless moments, I was just one among a gaggle of riders, elated after a hard and fast ride, sweating and laughing as we drank water from CamelBaks. No job titles. No politics. Just a few people speeding through the woods on high-tech mountain bikes.

It was through that lens—the way he pushed himself physically, the way he jokes, the way he shook it off after crashing on his bike—that I gained a different sense of the President's character. In my book, these kinds of moments are some of the most meaningful in life, and there is a certain unspoken camaraderie that didn't even need to be discussed. Both as my Commander in Chief and as a mountain biking buddy, I came to respect President Bush as a deeply kind, hilarious, and driven human being.

CHAPTER 7

KEEPING THE FLEET FLYING

During my first tour, I was a player in the complex chess game that HMX-1 operations represented. My role was perhaps that of a bishop or a rook. As CO, I was still a player, but I could see the whole chessboard on an entirely different and more strategic level. Not only did I have an entire HQ at Quantico, but we also maintained a secure facility at Anacostia. A lift package, ready to rock, and a contingent of my workforce rotated through Anacostia to keep the facility secure and operating 24/7/365.

Quantico is the heart of HMX-1's planning and helicopter maintenance, but Anacostia is where all planning becomes reality—where a mission briefed in the ready room becomes the sound of a helicopter starting, a pilot's hand on the stick, hovering above the airfield before gliding through the air en route to the White House or another locale.

Keeping the fleet flying was more than simply ensuring that the helicopters themselves were impeccably maintained. This was more like leading a highly complex orchestra with a thousand instruments, planning factors, and tasks to consider. I was the conductor of this structured symphony, this well-oiled machine that had not stopped running in more than fifty years. And although we made every effort to develop comprehensive and overlapping plans, and contingency plans, and emergency plans, world events actually dictated what the President might want to do, or when and where he might want to go—and therefore those events directly affected our daily operations.

We had some of the best of the best among our ranks, and the pursuit of excellence was viewed as standard operating procedure. I had a great staff and workforce that I would literally trust with my life. None of our success would have been possible without them. In fact, without the talented and dedicated people who showed up at Quantico and Anacostia every single day, HMX-1 would just be a really cool museum.

Still, the burden of responsibility fell on me. If there was any problem whatsoever with coordinating the President's helicopter support, or if *Marine One* ever failed to be in its preplanned location at exactly the right moment, or, God forbid, we ever had a flying accident or mishap, I would have to answer for it. Since I could not do everything or be everywhere at once, I had to trust my personnel implicitly. And I did.

Part of what made this kind of trust possible were the recurring, intensive efforts we made to recruit, hire, train, and retain the right people. All military units have what is called a Table of Organization (TOA), which lays out exactly how many and what types of positions are needed to run properly. In most Marine aviation squadrons, the staffing goal is 80 percent of the TOA. HMX-1 is one of fewer than five organizations that is authorized and required to maintain 100 percent staffing at all times.

I had personnel at virtually every level of the chain of command, including young kids who had enlisted right out of high school, seasoned pilots, and operations specialists. I had combat veterans and people from various locations and walks of life. Although we spanned the full range of organizational structure, experience, and functional areas—such as planning, operations, administration, security, communications, finance, training, recruiting, and more—I had to continuously focus my diverse workforce on shared goals. Every summer, a good percentage of the workforce got transferred when their four-year tour was up, so recruiting and training were perpetual planning factors.

As a result, one of the most important aspects of my annual schedule was traveling across the country with my internal recruiting team to various training facilities in search of talent. Of course, we did not expect to waltz in and grab all the best talent, but we made our best efforts to develop relationships and get as many as we could. My recruiting team included the maintenance chief, several senior enlisted members, a psychologist, and others.

The psychologist who helped us played a key role in identifying the right people. She also did recruiting for the Marine units that operated the White House ceremonial drill teams, and for a platoon of Marines that provided security at Camp David. It made perfect sense for her to help us, since those organizations had similar concerns as HMX-1. Think about it: the people we recruited would be working in a highly unusual environment, dealing with national assets and sometimes standing within feet of the President and other leaders. In that sense alone, it was similar to hiring a member of the Secret Service. They needed to have a certain type of psychological makeup for this kind of work, and we made sure to screen everyone thoroughly.

Even if we found a perfect candidate, we could never hire him if he failed the background checks for any reason. Typical Top Secret security investigations go back fifteen years into an individual's life. Our security clearances investigated the individual's entire lifetime. So even if a person thinks he got something expunged from his records, he is actually still judged by his past decisions and choices. Clearly, this stringent process leveled the playing field and shortened the list of potential candidates significantly. At the end of the day, we succeeded at maintaining a full-strength workforce in this dynamic environment, and the individual personnel were assigned to various organizational areas depending on their particular training and skill sets.

For example, on the pilot side of the house, my predecessor was leaving, and a couple of other *Marine One* pilots were nearing the end of their tours. I needed to start thinking about whom I was going to select as my backup *Marine One* pilots. We all had type-A personalities, and everyone wanted to be what only four people could ultimately become. I needed people who not only could fly but who could make split-second decisions even when chaos ensued. As I assessed my workforce and all the incredible talent surrounding me, my sights fell on Major Scotty Volkert. I knew him from Hawaii, and at the time he was assigned to HMX-1's Operational Testing and Evaluation mission. I wanted to make him my Operations Officer and one of my *Marine One* pilots. I knew he was a brilliant pilot with a good head on his shoulders.

I sat him down and told him about my plan for him. I would be increasing his workload, increasing his stress, and he would be away from home significantly more in his new role. After discussing the change with his family, he accepted the offer and became a member of my core team. This was one of the best decisions I ever made. Scotty was well respected and extremely meticulous in his planning and coordination. He is now a Lieutenant Colonel assigned to the White House Military Office's Airlift Operations Division, the organization that tasks *Marine One* and *Air Force One*.

Likewise, among the many personnel decisions and amazing people I worked with, one individual stands out as perhaps my best decision on the maintenance side of the house. I hand-selected Sergeant Harrison Kish to serve as the primary *Marine One* crew chief, and he never disappointed me once. In fact, he took support to a whole new level and did his job right 100 percent of the time. Sergeant Kish was a highly successful crew chief and participated on the vast majority of my Presidential lifts. Like many of his peers, he served honorably and then decided to leave the Marine Corps and go to college.

Planning and Operations

Planning is always central to military operations, with a constant flexibility to tweak the plan when conditions change (which they inevitably will). This was never more true than in HMX-1. The entire globe was our area of responsibility, current events informed our plans, and we did not have the luxury of shutting down the airfield or taking an operational pause. Ever. In my previous command back in Hawaii, there were a couple of times when I initiated a "safety stand-down." We didn't fly for about a week and instead focused on safety and other areas of concern.

This was a great leadership-and-training tool, but it was never an option at HMX-1. When the President was ready to go, my aircraft would be there and my crew chief would be standing like a statue beside the air stair, ready to salute. Period. I could make the decision not to fly the President if I felt he would be in danger, but that was rare. Normally, if the airfield at Anacostia was iced over, we simply had to integrate snowplows into the plan at the right time.

With such complex and intense mission sets, my operations planners were constantly thinking ahead to identify and mitigate risk. Under my direction, they developed and enforced strict processes and procedures to overcome human error and complacency. We did not get second chances. If anyone cut a corner or failed to follow procedure, especially if it caused some problem or safety issue, he or she was very likely to be fired and reassigned.

Another way to minimize risk is good old-fashioned military discipline. Every member of the workforce knew the rules and regulations, and of course they were strictly enforced by me and my subordinate leaders. But I also understand the ideology of teenagers. I had a standing order that I wanted to speak personally with every new member of the squadron. Sometimes this was one or more new personnel every week. My First Sergeant would sometimes wait until we had fifteen or twenty and then plan a time for me to meet with them all at once. My goal was to show them that I would be compassionate and understanding, and to express my pride at having them under my command.

I also wanted to give them a reality check. They were still kids, but they had to be absolutely devoted to the mission. I needed to make sure they understood the ramifications that simple life choices could have on their careers. Any infraction could be cause for dismissal.

I would often stand in front of them and ask, "By a show of hands, how many of you are under the age of twenty-one?" Most would raise their hands.

Next, I asked, "Okay, how many of you with your hands up have ever had a drink?" When, inevitably, only a couple of hands stayed up, I said, "Now you're lying," in a joking manner. They got the point. I went on to explain that when I grew up, eighteen was the legal drinking age, and that I didn't necessarily make the rules but I had to enforce them. I talked to them about the national importance of our mission and how critical every single person was to attaining that mission.

"You will work your ass off, and you will love it, and your parents will be proud," I would say, "but if you make a bad decision, or get caught drinking underage, you're gone. And it will follow you for your whole career in the Marine Corps." I certainly dealt with disciplinary issues at HMX-1, but not nearly as many as I had seen in previous assignments.

Because of the nature of our mission, security was a major planning factor and ongoing consideration. In previous assignments, there was always a contingent of security personnel, depending on the type of mission or operation. In my former command, my Marines often provided security support in a range of combat scenarios. At HMX-1, I had the largest MP company in the entire Marine Corps, comprised of more than one hundred personnel and dozens of canines. This highly professional group maintained 24/7/365 security of our HQ area, Anacostia, and also the lift package anytime it was on a mission. Just to make sure we had the place locked down tight, we sometimes got "visited" by certain White House assets to test our security and vulnerability.

The Cage

Never once in history has *Marine One* suffered a mishap, and this kind of record is almost unheard of in the military-aviation community, not to mention the private-aviation community. We can thank every member of the HMX-1 workforce for that. But perhaps we should give the biggest thanks to the mechanics, quality-control crews, and other aircraft experts. That corps of support personnel kept operations running while my pilots controlled the helicopters in the air. We always relied on the fact that the aircraft were always ready to go. And the hundreds of personnel that made up HMX-1's highly robust maintenance effort gave us that peace of mind.

There was no room for shortcuts when it came to maintenance, and any instance of malpractice would be another cause for dismissal. To mitigate this, we constantly refined the procedures, processes, and standards we used to ensure world-class maintenance. So, the most visible and famous helicopters in the world are also the most well maintained. HMX-1's rigorous standards of maintenance surpassed that of virtually any other helicopter on the planet. Why? We hold ourselves to a much higher maintenance standard than most aviation organizations. We fly the President.

We had an aggressive and perpetual inspection process that diminished complacency and sharpened preparedness and preventive main-tenance to a finer point. Another "secret" is that each aircraft is flown for a very specific and limited period of time. Every single part is then refurbished and checked, essentially resulting in having a brand-new aircraft at all times that is in a state of 100 percent maintenance and repair.

In any helicopter, there are static components (the piece of metal that makes up the rotor blade), and dynamic components (moving or spinning parts like a transmission or rotor head, or other hydraulics). All these parts have a service life that lets the maintenance folks know specifically when a part needs to be replaced or overhauled. An encyclo-pedic amount of documentation tracks a given part's time on the air-craft. Let's say that a dynamic component happens to have a service life of five hundred hours. In HMX-1, we cut that number in half, replacing or servicing the part twice as often as is required in a normal squadron.

The vital importance of maintenance can be seen in the fact that most of my workforce fell into that category. When the young mechan-ics, hydraulics specialists, and communications and systems specialists came to HMX-1 from one of the Marine Corps training facilities, we also put them through our own internal training. This was a gradu-ated process in which they spent a year or more working on the green-side aircraft before ever touching a white top. During this period, they learned how we did things, grew accustomed to the rhythm, and proved that they were ready to work on the white tops.

I also had seasoned maintenance leaders and quality assurance (QA) personnel. QA in this context is all about personal safety, aircraft safety, mechanical inspection, and maintenance-program auditing. In other words, QA provided ongoing supervision and oversight to all maintenance efforts, adding another layer of accountability and helping to ensure that the squadron is running the way that it is supposed to. Finally, the maintenance leadership is always assessing the workforce closely to determine which individuals will be assigned to which air-craft or shop, and which would be trusted to work in the highest and most classified level of HMX-1 maintenance: the Cage.

Physically, the Cage is a couple of hangars where HMX-1 mainte-nance takes place, and where the white tops are kept and maintained in pristine condition. Everyone who works in the Cage needs a Top Secret clearance, or else he is escorted by armed guards. Despite these points of distinction, in many ways the Cage is just like any other main-tenance operation. It is HMX-1's primary maintenance-management facility, and on any given day there might be a couple of hundred people working inside. It is the heartbeat of the maintenance effort for the executive fleet of aircraft.

As might be expected, the Cage is full of mechanics in work-soiled coveralls, aviator glasses, and steel-toe safety boots, with greasy hands from working in the tight, oily confines of the helicopter engines. One would also find the pungent smells of hydraulic fluid, oil, and cleaning solvent. The sounds of people talking and various power tools and avi-onics equipment fill the air. Sometimes I would come in from a mis-sion at night and walk through the hangar, talking to Marines on the night shift. There was a different vibe at these times, probably since maintenance was slow and there were fewer leaders on shift. I think the Marines on the night shift appreciated the time, and they would often have their music playing.

Although these were world-class maintenance personnel working on some of the most important and visible aircraft in the world, back then, we were stuffed into a hangar that was old and inadequate. They have since moved the Cage to a state-of-the-art facility, but back then, we were using the same hangars we had been using since the 1940s. It reminded me that the Marine Corps could adapt and overcome, doing so much with so little.

The *Marine One* Crew

With the plans perfectly dovetailed across every functional area, and when the moment came to fly the President where he wanted to go, I had to move the white noise of pressure and accountability into the proverbial backseat. I needed to be hyper-focused on the stick in my hand, the geography below, the weather, the architecture all around me, and on the singular goal of transporting the President safely to his destination. During those magical moments, I was just a pilot once again, and my "workforce" was distilled down to three: my copilot, my crew chief, and I.

The pilots and copilots certainly walked around the aircraft to do a visual inspection, and of course we were intimately familiar with the cockpit, but even we were discouraged from climbing on top of the aircraft and doing detailed inspections. This goes back to what I said about having complete trust in the processes and the people. When it came to maintaining the aircraft, we pilots and copilots respectfully stayed out of the way of the smart folks. Speaking of smart folks, no discussion about *Marine One*—or its ongoing inspection, maintenance, and upkeep—would be complete without mentioning the crew chief.

If the pilot and the copilot are the "brain" that keeps the aircraft flying, then the crew chief is the heart. And the *Marine One* crew chief is a little different from most crew chiefs. He's often considered the most photographed Marine in the world. In another sense, HMX-1 crew chiefs also served as the "face" of *Marine One*, since every time the President approached *Marine One*, and a camera shutter caught the moment, there was the crew chief standing like a statue beside the air stair. Not only do the crew chiefs take center stage in the images of *Marine One* that the world sees in photographs and videos, but they play an important role in ensuring that the helicopters are properly cared for and maintained.

This process begins when the potential crew chief completes boot camp and begins specialty training. There are four different schools required to become a CH-46 or CH-53 crew chief in the Marines, including three months of mechanic's training and six months of crew chief and flight training. After all that, a new crew chief can be selected for HMX-1, and then it's time for more training. Although there are variations to this scenario, a new crew chief might go through the following steps: first, he spends a year or two working on the green-side aircraft, learning about HMX-1 operations, and waiting for his Top Secret clearance to be complete. Once he gets the clearance, he may be selected to work on white tops, but typically only for Vice Presidential lifts and heads of state. Eventually, a crew chief may or may not be selected as a *Marine One* crew chief. At any given time, there are only four crew chiefs for each white-top model, and there is a constant turnover. Every few months, a new crew chief replaces an existing one, so there is always a "new guy" in learning mode, and a senior crew chief who mentors the others.

Not unlike my having to fulfill certain requirements before even being considered as HMX-1 CO, a *Marine One* crew chief must meet certain requirements. For example, an individual must complete the training to become a Collateral Duty Inspector (CDI). In the capacity of a CDI, the crew chief assists the QA personnel in inspecting maintenance efforts. They also had to meet certain standards on the physical fitness test and have a certain number of flight hours and Vice Presidential lifts. On top of all that, a crew chief had to be "voted on" by the peers in his respective maintenance shop.

Not only do the crew chiefs participate in any pre-flight rehearsals and preparation, but they play an important role during actual flight as well. The crew chief sits in the cockpit, between and a little behind the pilot and copilot seats. Among other things, the crew chief is constantly monitoring gauges, managing various internal and external lighting systems, the auxillary power unit, and the landing gears. Once *Marine One* lands, let's say on the White House lawn, the crew chief is already out of his seat and ready to spring into action.

The door that opens into the air stair on the VH-3 is quite heavy and must be lowered using only one rope, but the crew chiefs are well practiced in making it look smooth and easy. The door goes down and the crew chief catches it with his right hand and then sets it down gently on the lawn. The second the door is down, the crew chief starts walking ceremonially down the steps. Most Marines do drill only when they are back at their units. The *Marine One* crew chief performs highly ceremonial drill on every lift, and sometimes in front of the whole world (through the media). When he gets to the bottom of the steps, he takes eight steps out, pivots left, takes another eight steps, and another left. If it's a VH-3 on the lift, the crew chief opens the back door as well (where any other passengers will board). He then marches back the way he came to position himself right beneath the copilot's window and next to the air stair.

He may stand there for five minutes or an hour, and whether it's 10 below or a sweltering 110 degrees, the crew chief will stand there like a guard at Buckingham Palace, moving only after saluting the President as he boards. Approximately ten seconds after the President boards, the crew chief makes his way to the back door, then gets visual confirmation from the Secret Service that the President is securely on board. After getting the thumbs-up, he closes the back door and then walks back up the main steps and pulls the door closed behind him. Once the aircraft takes off, the crew chief is once again in his rightful place in the cockpit. Although the crew is a mere ten feet from the President and his guests, the only interaction happens either right before or after landing.

After landing back at Anacostia following a lift, and after the pilot and copilot turn over control of the aircraft, the crew chief still has a lot of work to do. Whether the lift lasted thirty minutes or all day, the crew chief (and possibly some of his fellow crew chiefs on shift) immediately performs a thorough aircraft inspection, cleaning, and preparation that could easily last three hours or much longer. Technically this process could be viewed as both pre- and post-flight procedures, since another lift could be planned at any moment, and this process was ongoing between all lifts. In other words, immediately following every lift, the aircraft had to be prepared for another one.

The inspection process involves a checklist with hundreds of entries and requires the crew chiefs to "touch" every part of the aircraft, inside and out. They check for visible damage, corrosion, breakage, and the service limitations on numerous parts on the engine, rotor head, tail, tiller head, the belly, and the interior. During the comprehensive inspections, the entire aircraft is also cleaned. The outside is washed and shined to maintain its high gloss. Cleaning the inside is treated with the same care. The cockpit windows are washed, the entire interior is vacuumed, and the seats and walls are cleaned with furniture polish. Snacks and beverages are replenished, according to the President's tastes. The crew chiefs even make sure the framed photos on the walls are straight, and that the seat belts are always positioned in the same way.

After all the cleaning and inspections are done, the crew chief finishes the associated paperwork. If any maintenance issues are identified during the inspection, the crew chief initiates a maintenance request and then physically assists in performing the maintenance. For instance, let's say a rotor blade needed to be changed out. The crew chief would help to change out the blade, then go back out for in-flight balance testing. Then they land, and QA tests the new blade again. If everything checks out with maintenance and QA, the crew chief might be able to go off shift for the day. But many times, they spent entire days testing, inspecting, retesting, and reinspecting to get a correct balance and measure on a replaced part. As if that wasn't enough, the crew chiefs have to be constantly prepared to present the most professional appearance, while providing the pilots with any pertinent follow-up information. Like I said, every single person in HMX-1 played an important role in overall operations, and the crew chief was at the very center of successful Presidential lifts.

Whether it's security, maintaining a trained and engaged workforce, ongoing planning and change management, personnel discipline, QA, or maintenance issues—there was simply no room for incompetence in HMX-1. Ultimately, I feel that I succeeded in forming and leading the right workforce, and we did not have any mishaps under my watch. I kept the fleet flying, as it were, and if HMX-1 continues to operate with enough vigilance and synergy, it should have another fifty years of operational excellence.

CHAPTER 8

FLYING THE COMMANDER IN CHIEF
AROUND THE GLOBE

Europe

Whether I was leapfrogging helicopters, equipment, and personnel on cargo planes and trains to ensure the right placement at the right time, or moving the entire lift package overseas, or simply flying *Marine One* in formation at a few hundred feet above countless American cities, it never got old. Despite the high pressure and immense responsibility that came with the job, the time away from home, and the seemingly endless amount of work that needed to be done in order to keep HMX-1 running, I never burned out, or looked forward to the end of my tour. If allowed, I would have gladly done a third tour.

As CO, I had the opportunity to travel all over the world with HMX-1. Sometimes I had to send one of my hand-selected *Marine One* pilots in my place, but I was on most of the trips. One of my favorite trips was flying the President all over Europe. He was going to meet with Angela Dorothea Merkel, the German Chancellor. After a few stops in Berlin, Poland, and the Ukraine, he would travel to London and meet with the Queen of England at Windsor Castle.

As usual, I collaborated with my Operations Department to develop the plan. Although VH-60s were much easier to transport overseas in cargo planes, this was a highly political and publicized trip, so I decided to bring VH-3s. I actually sent out three separate and complete lift packages, each comprised of all the right equipment and personnel. Two of the lift packages included VH-60s, which would support the President at the locations between Berlin and London. I would lead the primary lift package with the VH-3s, flying the President around Berlin, handing him off to *Air Force One* for the other short stops, and then flying the lift package to meet up with him in London.

Breaking down and configuring the VH-3s to fit into C-17s was a major undertaking from a logistical and maintenance perspective, and it was also a perishable skill since we didn't do it very often. I had a lot of experience within the Maintenance Department at that time, but there were also a number of personnel who had not yet taken VH-3s overseas. I was planning on doing the same thing for the D-day Sixty-fifth Anniversary event that I knew we would support with President Obama, and this mission was going to be a great training opportunity as well. It took an intensive maintenance effort to make the VH-3s fit into the C-17s. First of all, we used a crane to remove the entire white-top portion of the helicopter, which includes the engines and transmission. The WHLO would have to coordinate for similar cranes on the receiving end. The aircraft was still too tall to tow into the C-17. Next, the maintenance personnel had to install a different set of tires (we called them the training wheels) to shorten the height. Even after this, the VH-3 barely fit.

Once the helicopters were secured inside the C-17, we climbed up the back ramp and chose our spots on the cargo seating lining both sides of the aircraft. Our helicopters were right there in the middle of the massive space. We knew there was a lot of work ahead of us, and that we would probably get to see parts of a country we had not seen before. Once we rolled down the runway at Quantico, and pointed the nose of the aircraft to the east, there was a sense of calm before the storm. The flight across the Atlantic took six or seven hours, and once we reached altitude, everyone spread out

Since we traveled in the back of Air Force cargo planes a lot, everyone had a "C-17 kit," which usually contained creature comforts like a sleeping mat, snacks, books, movies, and anything else they wanted in there. The pilots switched to the red interior lights used in darkness, which create a soft and surreal ambience that just lulls you to sleep. And it's an unusual brand of C-17 sleep, where your pillow is gliding 30,000 feet above the ocean. People could be seen lying around on sleeping mats, watching movies on laptops, reading, and of course, sleeping.

I always changed into sweatpants for the flight, and relaxed on my sleeping mat as the massive bird flew silently over the dark waters below. It was a pretty nice way to travel, actually. Everyone knew when touchdown was getting close, so we packed up and prepared to get back to work. When that back ramp opened, everyone snapped into action to get the helicopters reconfigured.

According to our stringent maintenance and QA policies and procedures, certain things have to occur anytime the VH-3 is "deconstructed" to that level. Once the VH-3s are put back together under the close care of our maintenance and QA personnel, I had to fly it for ten hours before putting the President on the aircraft. Some of those hours would be burned off during a functional test flight, which is mandatory every time a dynamic component is removed. More of the ten hours would be burned off during rehearsals. But inevitably, I had to spend a couple of hours just flying around the countryside, doing our particular form of sightseeing. I wasn't complaining.

I had never been to Berlin before, so during rehearsals it was compelling to fly around the large industrial city, surrounded by vast countryside. While burning off the remaining ten hours, I even flew right over the place where the Berlin Wall once stood. When going overseas, we often don't pack up the green sides, or supporting aircraft. Instead, we coordinate with other U.S. military units nearby for support. In this case, a U.S. Army Black Hawk unit attached several helicopters and pilots to us all the way from Berlin to London. Although they were highly professional, HMX-1 is unlike any other organization. To overcome their lack of training in HMX-1 operations, I put one of my pilots and crew chiefs in each of the attached aircraft. The WHLO had done a great job in coordinating everything, and the rehearsals went off without a hitch as well.

At the appointed time, *Air Force One* landed and the President and the Chancellor climbed on board my aircraft. It was obvious from their body language that they were great friends. Among other stops, I flew them to their equivalent of our Camp David, called the Strauss. We landed next to a massive, regal building that looked like an old German villa with walls of soft, light pink, as if it had been built out of quartz. This main building and surrounding structures dotted a dense, old forest. Landing in a new place was always spectacular, and this day was especially exciting. The architecture, the trees, and just the whole affairs-of-state aura surrounding the event . . .

This was our head of state being hosted by another head of state, and as we flew across the countryside, we saw people lined up below to watch the green-and-white helicopters with the American flag and Presidential Seal on them. Although I was focused on the mission, in a sense we were putting on an international airshow in the German Chancellor's own backyard. The next day, I took the President back to *Air Force One*, and he headed out for the smaller trips that my other lift packages would support.

As I prepared to fly my own lift package across Germany and into London, I received daily and sometimes hourly updates about the status of the other lift packages. In the map of my mind, I could visualize all my assets operating across Europe. My route of travel would take me across Germany and the Netherlands, then over a corner of Denmark, into France, and then over the English Channel into London. I would fly us at a few hundred feet and at our normal cruising speed of 131 miles per hour.

A few hours in, we ran into some bad weather, and I had to make a decision to make an unscheduled stop in Europe, without clearance. I found a small airfield in the Netherlands, and we landed the entire lift package there. As soon as we got on the ground, I met with the airfield customs officials and called the White House Military Office. The right calls and coordination took place, and before long the weather cleared. We were all fueled up and ready to go.

The last leg of the trip was the most exciting for me. I had never been to that part of Europe before, and as an avid student of World War II, the vision in my mind was of a huge expanse of geography. I was amazed by how relatively small the area was. Conversely, the flight made me think about just how big our country is. In comparison, it would take me approximately three days (with the last day being pretty short) to fly from Washington, D.C. to California. Flying from Berlin to London took only the better part of one day.

More than anything else, my crew and I could not wait to see what the World War II pilots saw when they knew they had made it home safely—the White Cliffs of Dover. As we approached the English Channel, flying from the west coast of France toward the east coast of England, I saw the cliffs myself. I had flown the President over water before—off both coasts of the United States—but for the next twenty minutes I was almost rendered speechless as I flew *Marine One* across the Channel. I wasn't really speechless, because I was communicating with the air traffic controllers as I reached the far bank and flew up the river toward our destination—a military airfield north of London proper. Below me, I saw all those iconic buildings, including Tower Bridge, Big Ben, and Buckingham Palace.

Once we landed in London, I began the preparation and coordination for several full-scale rehearsals. I had to work with the English security organizations, including security around the Royal Family, their military police, and their civilian police. Everything had to be perfect. A couple of days later, and after rehearsal landings at Windsor Castle, the President arrived. I was sitting on the runway at Heathrow International Airport, watching *Air Force One* barrel toward me. That first day, I flew the President to his temporary residence.

On the second day of his visit, I flew the President to Windsor Castle for tea and lunch with the Queen. The flight took approximately the same length of time as it took me to fly from the White House to Camp David (about forty minutes). I flew right over little hamlets and old churches dotting the landscape beneath us. This did not look or feel anything like the United States, especially when I saw what I thought were fairly large castles and medieval estates. I was sure I wasn't in the United States any longer when I saw the size of Windsor Castle, a five-hundred-person estate that is actually the largest occupied castle in Europe.

When we landed, the Secret Service had a motorcade waiting to transport the President to his meeting with the Queen. While President Bush sipped tea with the Queen, I remained with the aircraft on the lawn, going over the communications channels, checking in with my pilots and our liaisons from the Secret Service, and mentally rehearsing the order of takeoff.

He returned exactly two hours later and was smiling as he walked from the motorcade to *Marine One*. He stopped in the cockpit for a moment, slapped me on the back reassuringly as we started to take off, and said, "Frenchman, try not to hit the castle."

I flew the President back to *Air Force One* and watched him take off. Another mission complete.

North America

Flying a helicopter, even in HMX-1, could never be assumed to be 100 percent safe. Parts can fail. Natural disasters can occur. Helicopters can crash. Of course, none of these things had ever happened at HMX-1, and I did not plan on them happening under my watch, but they could.

Obviously, President Bush was certainly a desirable target for many terrorist groups. Although we took precautions (and all of them are highly classified), flying *Marine One* could be considered dangerous in its own way.

And while *Marine One* was certainly not a first responder by any means, it was still the President's preferred method of travel. This meant that when natural disasters or national emergencies occurred, he wanted us to get him there fast. Really, all of HMX-1 operations required rapid planning and a high operations tempo, but national situations kicked it up a notch.

In August 2007, a bridge collapsed on I-35 near Minneapolis and St. Paul, Minnesota, killing a dozen people and injuring more than a hundred. I didn't know any of this right away because I was in the auditorium at Quantico when it happened. Although we couldn't do "real" safety stand-downs as I had at the Ugly Angels, even HMX-1 was mandated to do some kind of safety stand-down. To the degree possible, I had assembled some of the workforce for one day of safety briefings.

During a break, I received a call from my Operations Officer.

"Sir, a bridge collapsed in Minnesota. It's not good. We just got the call from the White House, the President wants to be there tomorrow."

I had to get a package of aircraft out there that same night. When the group returned from the break, I alerted them to the situation and said, "Okay, here's what we're going to do. We need a lift package in Minneapolis tonight for a lift tomorrow. Anyone that is needed to make that happen, you know who you are. Go, now. The rest of you, we'll finish the briefings."

A few dozen folks made their way out, and I looked at the rest of them and said, "This exemplifies why we are here today. The mission never stops, but we can still pause and discuss safety when we can."

I got back to Quantico just an hour or two later, met up with my crew, packed up, and flew the entire lift package to Minneapolis. The President was going to meet with state officials, then he wanted to fly to and land right near the bridge and see the destruction for himself.

I brought two VH-60s and three CH-53s, as I knew there would be a lot of press. All the support personnel and gear would travel by C-130 and meet us there. After a five-hour flight across the nation's heartland, flying over the Shenandoah and Ohio valleys, and making two quick fuel stops, we landed at an Air National Guard base that was part of the Minneapolis–Saint Paul airport.

I immediately linked up with my WHLO, and spoke with the White House press personnel, who wanted to get a shot of the President flying over the bridge in *Marine One*. I coordinated to have the photographer in one of my support aircraft. I then told the pilot of that aircraft that when the time came for the shot, he could just direct me over our internal radio frequency.

That night, I watched the news coverage of the collapsed bridge, which was now close by. I felt so bad for the families affected. This was one of those somber missions. The next morning, *Air Force One* landed at the airfield, and the President climbed aboard my aircraft.

I lifted off and headed straight to the bridge. Coordinating everything over the various communication channels, I took him in at just a couple of hundred feet. The images from the news the night before were now vivid below me. This was an active emergency scene. Some of the victims had still not been accounted for. The bridge, which normally spanned the Mississippi River, was now submerged in the water. I could see huge blocks of concrete, rebar or some other kinds of exposed metal, cars and trucks in the water, and a school bus caught up against one railing. Rescue boats were nearby. There was an intact bridge right next to the collapsed one, creating a disturbing before-and-after rendering.

I circled the scene several times to let the President get a good look. I was a pilot first and foremost, using all my experience to provide the safest flight possible for the President. I was also aware that the whole world was watching through the lens of the media. I also spoke with one of my pilots about the photograph. We got that taken care of, and I headed over to the predetermined landing zone on the bank of the river.

My WHLO had coordinated for us to land in a field right near the bridge. The choreography of this particular landing was tricky, because the CH-53s (Night Hawks 3 and 4) were carrying the press, and they had to land before the President. Typically, we would all touch down in the same landing zone, but this one was not large enough. In a highly synchronized set of maneuvers, the two CH-53s landed and their passengers disembarked. I then brought the President in and shut the aircraft down, and it quickly became a secure area.

The President toured the site with officials and spoke with some of the rescue workers. Because we were already inside the secure area, we were allowed to walk right up to the precipice of the collapsed bridge. It was a frightening view from that vantage point, and the area of the bridge that was once over land now looked like some concrete ramp ready to launch vehicles into the water. We tracked the President's movements and were ready to take off when he returned to *Marine One*.

Later that night, I was back in my hotel room, watching HMX-1 in action on the evening news. When the President was safely back in *Air Force One* the next day, and I was flying into the sun back to Quantico, I felt a great sense of accomplishment. We had made the whole thing work, but it had taken a lot of people jumping through hoops. This had been an unscheduled, rapid-planning trip, and we had operated outside of normal operating procedures with the landing zone. I was proud of us. The President wanted to react to an emerging situation, and we had made it seamless for him. Not too many aviation units in the world could have pulled that one off.

During my tenure, we performed several other similar missions, such as when tornadoes hit the Midwest, and the California wildfires. In each case, we worked together as a massive organization focused on a shared goal. The President was exactly where he wanted to be—showing his support to those affected by the disasters—exactly when he wanted to be there. On a personal level, I felt deeply for those people, and saw firsthand what the swath of destruction of a major tornado looked like from 200 feet. I remember how odd it seemed that it was such a clear and beautiful day, but just days before we arrived, Mother Nature had scoured the earth.

In between these kinds of lifts, there were also numerous planned lifts. Most of these were a perfect combination of hard work and fun. We prepared in the way that only HMX-1 could, and then carried out our mission. If we had a little downtime, some destinations were more fun than others. New York City was a favorite destination for everyone in the squadron. I had made the trip dozens of times, and in 2008 I flew the President there for the United Nations convention. International allies, foreign dignitaries, and military and government officials would be descending on the city from around the globe, adding an unusual flavor to the overall mission.

We planned out the mission specifics back at Quantico, including contingency plans and pilot and crew selection. We would fly the lift package from Quantico to JFK International Airport, in Queens. There, we would link up with *Air Force One* and then transport the President to Manhattan. As chance would have it, the National Geographic Channel was filming a show called *Onboard Marine One*, and parts of this trip were featured in the show. So, along with all the normal planning factors, we actually integrated National Geographic camera crews and other personnel into our plans.

We arrived a few days early and began rehearsals. Peter Schnall, the National Geographic producer, asked if we could get some aerial shots. I happily agreed and took him up for a flight over Central Park. We took off from JFK and made our way across the city. There was a lot more helicopter traffic in and around Manhattan than usual. It is always a treat to fly smoothly between the buildings of New York City, getting a glimpse of the swimming pools, gardens, and even tennis courts on top of some of them. There's also something really special about flying over Central Park, that green expanse that breaks up the otherwise dominant architecture of the massive city. Peter got the footage he wanted, which I enjoyed later when the show was aired.

On the morning of the convention, I gathered everyone around me in a large, open hangar at JFK. There were about seventy pilots and support personnel in flight suits, standing in a semicircle. I gave one final safety briefing, then said, "Nobody can do it better than us. Let's get it done. And yes, we are in Manhattan, so enjoy yourselves. Any questions?"

I knew that one of my white tops had picked up the President at the White House that morning at the designated time and transported him to Andrews, where he boarded *Air Force One* for the trip to New York City. Like clockwork, we climbed into our aircraft to wait for the President's arrival. Once on board, I flew him to the Wall Street heliport, which is a narrow strip of concrete jutting out into the East River.

I called for clearance from air traffic control, then dropped down and flew in at a low altitude, heading west right along the shore. Coney Island was below us, teeming with people all over the boardwalk. Some of them waved as we flew overhead. Roller coasters and other amusement park rides look very different from the air. We hit the tip of Coney Island, turned right, and flew right between the left and right stanchions of the Verrazano-Narrows Bridge, which connects Staten Island and Brooklyn.

Now I aimed the formation toward the tip of Manhattan, with the Statue of Liberty to the left and Governor's Island on the right. Approaching that iconic skyline from the south, the first thing I always noticed was the absence of the World Trade Center. During my first tour the towers had still been standing. We came in for the final approach to the Wall Street heliport. I had sent my WHLO team in to carefully designate where each helicopter would land. They were wearing suits (business casual) rather than their Marine uniforms, so as not to draw attention. I could see them below us, blending in with the Secret Service, the U.S. Coast Guard, local law enforcement, and other security personnel awaiting our arrival.

This landing could be tricky. If the winds were coming from the north, it was not too bad, much like landing on a ship. If the winds were out of the south, though, then I would have to head toward the Brooklyn Bridge, do a 180-degree turn, and fly right over the top of the other helicopters before landing. Luckily, the winds were coming in from the north on this particular morning.

I directed the other aircraft to land first, then took *Marine One* in for the final descent. The heliport was packed with people and aircraft, but I had landed in tight spaces before. When we were safely on the heliport, the President was whisked away in his motorcade under incredibly tight security. He was actually there for the whole weekend, and the next day we flew him to a school yard in New Jersey for a local event. As always, when the mission came to an end, we linked up with *Air Force One*, then made our way home and began preparing for the next mission.

The Boss Says Goodbye

In late 2008, President Bush was approaching the end of his second and last term. I knew firsthand how much he appreciated his military, and HMX-1. Still, he certainly wasn't expected to do anything special to let us know that. As he had so many times since I had met him, he surprised me.

In his last months in office, President Bush made an unprecedented trip to our hangar at Quantico to express his gratitude personally. No other President in history had ever visited Quantico to thank the members of HMX-1.

The President's visit to Quantico was a very big deal for us. The same kind of security measures were executed on that base regarding his arrival and transporting actions. The morning of his visit, the hangars had been prepared, and the Secret Service had carried out their usual checks and sweeps. I told my entire workforce to be in the hangar at the right time.

Meanwhile, I picked up the President for one of the very last times on the White House lawn. This mission was different. I was picking him up at his home, and on that day I felt like I was bringing him to my home-away-from-home. Imagine getting to bring the President of the United States home for a visit.

Right on time, he walked out of the South Portico and boarded *Marine One*. He came up into the cockpit and said, "Frenchman, how you doing today?"

"I'm doing great, sir."

"I guess you know the way we're going, right?"

I laughed. "Yes, sir, I got it."

I flew him first to the FBI Academy at Quantico, where he addressed the graduating class. I then flew him five minutes across Quantico to the HMX-1 compound. Normally I would be out on the landing strip, but on this day I landed right in front of the hangar filled with my beloved Marines. Another difference this day was that, while I usually stayed put in the cockpit until the President had exited the aircraft, this time I got off the aircraft, too, which felt kind of strange.

It was one of those really cold days, and the hangar doors were shut to keep the heat it. There were some members of the media just outside the hangar, but they knew the President was just saying goodbye, so they weren't actually part of the event. As we approached, someone cracked the hangar doors about two feet wide so that we could walk through the opening.

Inside, more than eight hundred pilots, mechanics, and administrative, communications, logistics, and other personnel were arrayed in a large semicircle. When I walked in with the President, the group immediately exploded into a loud roar of applause and yelling. Goose bumps jumped up on my neck, because I did not anticipate this kind of reception. It was like a rock star had just entered the premises. I could see it in their eyes. They were utterly motivated by the sight of their Commander in Chief and their own Commanding Officer.

As we made our way to the small stage and podium that had been set up, my Sergeant Major commented to me that this was an inappropriate reception. "Sir," he said, "this is their Commander in Chief. They should be standing at attention." I said, "Nah, not today, Sergeant Major. He loves it."

The media tried to rush the hangar to capture this spirited reception, but the Secret Service kept them at bay outside. President Bush and I walked up onto the stage together, and I looked out at my workforce. Their faces were beaming. These were the people who enabled HMX-1 to fulfill its mission on a daily basis, and without them none of it would have been possible. I saw Bayou and Spanky out in the crowd, clapping almost as hard for me as for the Commander in Chief.

As I waited a few minutes for the screaming and cheering to simmer down, I realized that this was the only time in my life I would ever have the chance to introduce the President of the United States. I walked up to the microphone and said, "Good morning, HMX-1." More cheering.

I then looked directly at the President and said, "It's an honor to have your here, sir. It's not lost on me that this is the first time any President has ever entered this hangar, even though it's been standing since Harry Truman was in office." This got a few laughs from the crowd and a smile from the President. I then turned to the crowd and said, "He obviously needs no introduction from me, but I am proud and honored to introduce our Commander in Chief."

There was even more roaring applause as the President came forward and gave a short and moving speech. His words were very heartfelt, as he thanked us sincerely for all that we had done for him and his family. He thanked us for our service and dedication and for serving our country in uniform. He made some comments about how many lifts we had done during his presidency and said that he understood and appreciated the constant and hard work that went on behind the scenes.

It felt like my role as Commander of HMX-1 and my friendship with the President joined on that stage, as I stood next to my boss and friend with my Marines watching. After his speech we presented him with a few tokens of our appreciation. First, we presented him with the glass from the very window of *Marine One* that he had looked out of so many times. What thoughts had he cast through that glass?

We had mounted the glass on a nice plaque and had engraved on it FAIR WINDS AND FOLLOWING SEAS. This was a common phrase used in Marine hail-and-farewell ceremonies, and had been passed down through history as a nautical phrase of good luck for the person heading out on his new "voyage." The squadron logo also adorned the plaque.

Next, we presented him with a tail rotor blade from *Marine One*. Our paint shop had finished the blade with a high-gloss paint, making it look like the white tops themselves. That was mounted on a plaque as well. Even though he appreciated the gifts, as I knew he would, I wanted to do something even more personalized and special.

In the weeks preceding the event, I had come up with the idea of designing a *Marine One* bicycle helmet. I bought a nice helmet and asked Lance Corporal Meekins to paint it in the *Marine One* theme. He was a very talented and artistic young man, and I knew he could do it justice. He accepted the challenge, taped everything up, and then painted it perfectly in several layers. The end product was gorgeous, and absolutely unique.

The President was thanking us for the other gifts when I said, "We have something else for you, Boss." I then had Lance Corporal Meekins come forward and present President Bush with the helmet. The smile on the President's face while I explained the images on the helmet said it all—he loved it.

I honestly thought that once he made his remarks, he would do an about-face, and we would head back out of the hangar and get him back to the White House. Instead, he spent an hour taking photos and shaking hands with as many people as he could. This caused an even bigger frenzy, because collectively we were all so grateful for his show of gratitude.

I was kind of following him around, just soaking it all in, when he suggested that we take a group picture. The White House photographer stood on a work stand and took the shot of the entire squadron in a semicircle, with the President right in the middle. Of course, there was a point in time when I had to get back into the aircraft and start it up for the flight back to the White House. I coordinated this with the military aide, and was in my pilot seat when the President walked out to *Marine One*.

He leaned into the cockpit again and said, "Frenchman, thank you so much for that. That was great. That was just awesome." I flew the aircraft back up the Potomac to the White House lawn, and my crew and I were still reeling from the energy in the hangar. We dropped him off and headed back to Quantico once more.

I was beyond appreciative that the President had recognized my Marines like that. It made what they do every day even more real for them. I was giddy by the time I got back to the HQ, and my Sergeant Major looked at me and said, "Sir, I have to tell you. You shined today."

The next time I flew the President to Camp David was one of the last visits, and one of the last excursions for Peloton One. We met up in the morning and, sure enough, he was wearing the helmet.

Everyone noticed it and commented on how cool it was. The President was just looking at me, beaming, and saying proudly without a beat, "Yep! This is my *Marine One* helmet. It's my new favorite helmet."

It was a fairly typical and strenuous ride, and afterward we were cooling down in front of the President's cabin.

He looked at me innocently and said, "Frenchman, I love the helmet so much, but I need a size bigger."

"Roger that, sir." I smiled as I rode away, because the President obviously thought we had a gift shop at the squadron. We hadn't told him how much we had put into it, and he didn't realize that it was one-of-a-kind. I wasn't going to tell him. I took the helmet back to Lance Corporal Meekins, and he agreed to do another one, no problem.

What is it that is so enthralling about serving a President in such a direct, personal way? First of all, the immense pride and sense of privilege that comes with serving the President cannot be understated. The access to the most powerful man on the planet and the daunting responsibility of my role were not lost on me, either. But it wasn't just the "star quality," because I had become accustomed to interacting with famous or powerful people long ago. So what was it? Why did Corporal Meekins smile, nod, and so diligently create another helmet? Why did I savor my work for the President like no other job before or since? Why did we all work so hard to support him?

Maybe it was the access to the inner circle of the highest levels of our government. You can watch movies with a White House theme, watch the news, even watch reruns of *The West Wing* and marvel at what it must be like. But living it day to day for a couple of years gave me an education and an opportunity that will stick with me for life. I felt so lucky every time I entered the White House with the credentials I had, because of the job I had. From the first to the last time I went into the White House—walking alone from the East Wing to the West Wing, looking at portraits and photographs, the plates displayed in the China Room, the murals in the Diplomatic Reception Room, nodding in recognition to staff members and Secret Service members, or just pausing at the Rose Garden as I walked down the West Wing Colonnade—I never lost the "holy shit!" feeling that I was part of a small minority of Americans who had the privilege to do and see these things.

On another level, maybe it was the unique flying role. In the aircraft, the sense of privilege and responsibility took on a whole new dimension. For a few moments in time, I was charged with the safety and security of the President of the United States. Every time I strapped that aircraft on and sat at the ready, waiting for the President to climb aboard, I uttered the small but extremely relevant "Alan Shepard prayer" that all pilots learn and have uttered many times: "Please, Lord . . . do not let me fuck this up." And on yet another level, there was a sense of privilege and exclusivity that came with spending weeks on Camp David. Although it was my job to be there, we were still treated as guests of the President at a little green patch on the planet that feels like paradise. Whether I was mountain biking, sitting in the chow hall, or hanging out in my cabin, I knew that "paradise" was surrounded by an intensely secured airspace, which we called the "doughnut of death" for those who would try to penetrate it without approval.

Or maybe the magic was in the faces of friends, family, and the public, when they heard about my job. I could always read the wow factor in their faces, especially when meeting someone for the first time. I think all these different aspects of flying the President coalesced into an unforgettable and very fulfilling experience. I always tried to find the right balance of humility, while believing at a very deep and personal level that I seriously had the coolest job in the world.

Inauguration Day 2009

The buildup to the January 2009 Inauguration began weeks in advance. As commander of HMX-1, I had sole responsibility for orchestrating helicopter support for the event, which included rehearsals and extensive coordination with the White House staff, the Inauguration Committee, the Secret Service, and dozens of other military and civilian contacts.

By the Friday before the Inauguration, the squadron, support, and security were all in place. Since President Bush and his family spent that last weekend at Camp David, that's where I spent the weekend as well. It was pretty cold when we took our final ride the Sunday morning before the inauguration, and we didn't get to talk much in what the President called a "balmy twenty degrees."

I returned the President and his family to the White House on Sunday evening and flew back to my headquarters at Quantico. I lived only a few miles from base, and falling asleep that night was a challenge to say the least. I jumped out of bed early on the morning of the Inauguration, already running through the day's procedures in my head while I was brushing my teeth. It was going to be a day of rich American history and tradition, and I had a front-row seat. I wanted to make sure that I gave President Bush a real send-off. I had so much admiration for the man, and I just wanted to do my small part to be supportive during what must have been a very emotional morning.

While the past and future Presidents of the United States and their families were no doubt waking and stirring about with nervous excitement and anticipation, my crew and I warmed up *Marine One* and took it for a spin around Washington, D.C. The horizon was nothing more than a thin sliver of light just starting to burn away the deep blue sheet of the sky. I looked out at the city lights in every direction and took the aircraft slow and low over the city.

It was maybe 5:30 A.M., but the city was not asleep. The National Mall was all lit up, and people were already camping out even though the Inauguration Ceremony would not begin until noon. I had to be in place at the Capitol by 7:00 A.M., so I headed back to base to make my final preparations. We realized that the heater unit was malfunctioning, and of course that would not do. So, in the hours before the Presidential Inauguration, we switched white tops. Of course we had plans for this type of contingency, and we had other white tops ready, for the most part. Still, it's not the type of thing you want to do on a morning like that.

I did a final briefing before we headed back downtown. Every single *Marine One* mission was treated with the utmost importance, and our job was the same no matter who the President or what the event. Still, the gravity of the day was not lost on any of us as I gave a detailed mission briefing about our flights, security, and other planning, made all the more complex by the events of the day and the size of the crowd.

By the time I took off again to position *Marine One* for the Inauguration Ceremony, D.C. was absolutely brimming with activity. On the morning of a Presidential Inauguration, it is traditional for the outgoing President and the First Lady to host the incoming President and new First Lady. While the Bush family was hosting the Obama family in the White House, probably having coffee or a light breakfast, I flew over D.C. toward the Capitol, sipping my own cup of coffee from the machine in my office.

The streets were clogged with traffic, and even more people were pouring into the National Mall. I flew over the Lincoln Memorial and landed very close to the Capitol steps—something that can happen only during an Inauguration. People were cheering and waving as cameras flashed. The Capitol was decorated in patriotic colors and the glowing interior lights were framed by the crisp blue sky.

I had hand-selected a team of four that morning: myself; my co-pilot, Captain Chris Roy; my crew chief, Sergeant Harrison Kish; and one of my security Marines, Sergeant Jordan Hardy, who was already at the Capitol to keep the landing site secure. We walked up the steps and into the Capitol with almost five hours until we took off again for the final flight to Andrews Air Force Base. But with all the activity behind the scenes, those hours went by like minutes.

I was obviously focused on the operational side of things. *Marine One* had been providing Presidents with impeccable support for more than fifty years, and I had every intention of carrying on that tradition today. But I was also immersed in the personal and historical side of the event. I walked out to the same rotunda where past Presidents had stood, and where our future President would be standing in just a few hours. I looked out at the Mall and got yet another incredible perspective of the enormous crowd that had swelled even more since my pre-dawn flight.

Just downstairs from the rotunda, an executive office had been designated for those of us behind the scenes. I grabbed another cup of coffee and watched the media coverage of the event on a TV nearby. Watching the news, I knew those cameras were just outside the building, pointed right at us. I spent the next few hours talking to colleagues and associates, going out to warm up the helicopter every hour or so, and generally trying to stay out of the way. The press was poised, so even my warming up the engines became something to report. Each time I went back into the building and sat down, I saw on the news what I looked like from everyone else's perspective. I knew that my parents were watching with pride.

Eventually, dignitaries like Congressmen, Senators, Justices, family members, and other VIPs began to arrive and be seated for the event. I monitored the radio to track the President's movements. It was reflex. It was my job to know where he was, to know where he wanted to go, and then to take action to get him there. On TV, I saw the Obamas climbing into a motorcade for the trip from the White House to the Capitol. Next, I saw the Bushes, and I knew that it wouldn't be long until it was go time.

When the actual Inauguration of our forty-fourth President finally began, I was glued to the TV just like anyone else. The only difference was that I was right behind those walls. As President Obama finished his speech, I looked at my crew and said, "Okay, boys, giddy up."

When we walked out to the aircraft this time, the crowd started roaring. They had gotten as close as possible to the Capitol without entering the secure area, and were taking thousands of photos. I walked up the steps, took a look around the cabin, and climbed into the warm cockpit. Sergeant Kish was out there, standing at attention in the bitter cold.

As I sat there waiting for the Bush family to board, I had yet another great perspective. I had been part of so many military and Presidential speeches and ceremonies, but nothing as important and steeped in tradition as this. The stairs of the Capitol were lined with military personnel in dress uniforms when three iconic couples in long winter coats came into view and began to descend: the Bushes, the Obamas, and the Bidens. They all stopped at the bottom of the stairs and exchanged pleasantries.

Around this time, President Bush 41 and Barbara Bush approached the steps. It was clear that he was struggling as his wife helped him up the stairs. He had aged a lot since we played walleyball all those years ago.

Once inside, he put his hand on my shoulder, smiled, and said, "It's tough getting old," then laughed and took his seat.

Jenna and Barbara Bush and Jenna's husband boarded the aircraft next. I turned and greeted them as they did, and I could sense their energy and excitement. Finally, the man who had been the President of the United States until just a few moments earlier made his way toward my aircraft. Laura Bush entered first, as the President turned and waved to the crowd and to the Obama and Biden families, who were waving from the Capitol steps.

I had also gotten to know Laura quite well during all my time at Camp David and the Crawford ranch. True to her days as a teacher and a true southern lady, Laura looked at me with that warm and friendly smile she always had. "Good morning," she said.

"Good morning, ma'am."

She made her way back to sit down with her family. I had the stomach butterflies when President Bush finally boarded *Marine One*. I'm not sure what I was expecting, but as he came up to the cockpit to greet us, he looked more exuberant and content than I had ever seen him before. He grinned as he put his hand on my shoulder and said, "Frenchman, let's go."

"Roger that, Boss." The engines had been running, and now I started to spin the rotors. Outside, the crowd went wild.

It was an exercise in personal discipline to remain focused on the task at hand in the excitement of the moment, as I lifted gently off the east side of the Capitol and began a very slow circle over the frenzied chaos below.

Even though my job description didn't change from President to President, I still felt a sense of loss that morning. I had ridden mountain bikes with President Bush so many times I had lost count, and I had gotten to know him so much more than I ever would have imagined. I had flown him to locations all over North America, South

America, Europe, and Asia, but the grand adventure was coming to an end today. He was moving on, and I would be retiring soon.

The night before, I had written him a note:

Sir, it has been my honor and privilege being your helicopter pilot for the last couple of years. I've enjoyed every moment of serving you, and riding with you . . . you will always be MY President.

Semper Fi,

The Frenchman

I placed the note on the President's seat before the flight, but I didn't know if he would read it right then or tuck it into his jacket pocket for later. As I circled the crowd for the second time, one of the aides called me on the helicopter's internal radio system and said, "Colonel L'Heureux, he just read your note. He seems really moved by it."

That was the first time the White House photographer had ever flown in my aircraft, but his timing couldn't have been better that morning. I found out later that as the President looked down at the Capitol and the massive crowd below him with my note in his hand, the photographer snapped a picture.

I had been in so many historical flights, but I doubt that more eyes were ever on me than at that moment. Every President is supposed to get a final flight in *Marine One*, but President Clinton's had been canceled due to inclement weather. The last time this historical "victory lap" had taken place had been sixteen years ago. I had been a young Captain watching my Commander fly President Bush 41. Today, I was the Commander, and I was flying both generations.

Vice President Cheney was in a wheelchair that day and traveling in a separate aircraft to Andrews Air Force Base. He had to arrive before us, because he was supposed to introduce the President. It was traditional to fly around the Mall, but I was also buying time.

I called over the radio to get a status update: "This is *Marine One*. Any word on the location of the Vice President?"

"Roger, still en route."

He still wasn't there. *Slower, Frenchy, slower.*

I was starting to worry. I was on my third lap over the crowd, but you don't just keep flying the President and his family around without good reason. I made another radio call and learned that the Vice President was finally getting close. I turned to the east and flew away from the crowd and toward Andrews Air Force Base. After only a couple of minutes, I landed right at the nose of *Air Force One* and shut down the rotors. Usually, I would remain in the cockpit until the First Family left the aircraft, then climb down and start the post-flight procedures. This was the last time the Boss would be leaving my aircraft, and the emotion of the moment was upon me. I wanted to remember it.

I got out of my seat and stood inside the aircraft near the top of the stairs. I exchanged hugs with everyone on board, until only Laura and President Bush remained. Laura came up first, wearing a large black coat. She gave me perhaps the warmest smile I have ever received, and then we hugged and she said, "Thank you for taking such good care of my family these years."

"My pleasure, ma'am."

As she went down the stairs, President Bush approached me with his own warm and knowing smile. I tried to come up with something poignant to say, as all the memories we'd shared over the past few years flashed by in my head. I think he could tell I was struggling with the words.

He just walked right up to me and gave me a big hug. I hugged him back. He said, simply, "I'm going to miss you."

"I'm going to miss you, too," I said, and he walked off *Marine One* for the last time. As he descended the steps, he was greeted by yet another crowd.

I walked over to *Air Force One* and climbed the steps. I greeted the security guard and walked up to the cockpit to talk with Colonel Mark Tillman, my counterpart and the pilot of *Air Force One*. I knew that the day was a big deal for him, too, because he was retiring from the Air Force right around the same time as President Bush left office. After talking with Mark about what it felt like to fly President Bush for the last time, I went into the hangar where the President's speech was about to begin.

I was surrounded by hundreds of people I had come to know so well over the past couple of years. When the speech ended, there was security and a rope line to contain the crowd. I was milling around near the hangar doors, talking to some colleagues, when the President and his family made their way to the steps of the 747.

Throngs of people were trying to get their attention, and in their typical way they stopped to talk to most of them. They shook hands and exchanged hugs with all the well-wishers, and I just stood there smiling broadly. I had already said my goodbyes, and my crew had done an amazing job at the Inauguration. It was another touching moment, and I was proud of President Bush.

At that moment, the President caught my eye. He walked right over to me before boarding the plane. While the crowd watched and cheered, he just smiled at me again, then put his hand on top of my head and tousled my hair, like a dad congratulating his son after a good game. I caught a couple of bemused looks from people standing close-by.

They climbed the stairs, waved, and boarded the aircraft. The plane began to taxi down the runway. As it took off and headed south and west toward Crawford, Texas, I felt the weight of the day leave me.

A few weeks later, I received a letter in the mail dated just before the Inauguration, on White House letterhead. It reads:

> A Prime Minister, a NATO head, ambassadors, cabinet secretaries, and a mayor.
> A general, chopper pilots, Camp David chargers, military vets, mil aides, and doctors.
> Family, White House family, campaign vets, Fellows, agents, advance dudes, photo dogs, and a State Department "chick."
> Pro racers, bike fitters, bike builders, trail builders, and a noted author.
> Bike company owners, entrepreneurs, executives, and a head coach.
> Amputees, Olympians, 24 hour racers, reporters, radio talkers, and a mailman.
> E Pluribus Unum—out of many = <u>Peloton One.</u>
> Thanks for the memories,
> George Bush

Along with the letter was another pair of biking socks, but this time they had the Presidential Seal with PELOTON ONE around it, and below that: PELOTON ONE—FINAL EDITION. I still had an important job to do, and I could only hope that my new boss would be as gracious, kind, and warm as this one had been. I soon met President Obama, and my final chapter with HMX-1 began.

Meeting the Obamas

The day after the Inauguration, I had a meeting at the White House to meet my new boss (Louis Caldera, the Director of the White House Military Office). He had served as Secretary of the Army under President Clinton, and he wanted to meet with all the Directors and Commanding Officers under his scope of responsibility.

I arrived early so that I had time to walk through the White House for a few minutes. I grabbed a cup of coffee, then stopped by to chat with the Director of the Secret Service, who had become a friend of mine. I then made my way back through the West Wing and ran into Colonel Tillman. His replacement, and my new counterpart, Colonel Scott Turner, was also there.

We talked for a few moments, right near the stairs where the Situation Room and the entrance to the Press Room are located. We were preparing to walk back to the East Wing when I saw the Secret Service guys coming through. I knew by their body language that the President was very close by. We just kind of backed up to the wall to make way, and President Obama and Vice President Biden came around the corner. They both seemed in high spirits as they introduced themselves to people. Then suddenly they were heading right at us. We were all wearing suits that morning, which we always did unless it was a designated uniform day or we had a lift.

When National Geographic had filmed President Obama on *Air Force One*, Scott was the pilot. Obama looked at Scott with a friendly smile and said, "I know you."

Scott said, "Yes, sir, you do."

The President then extended his hand to me and said, "Hi, how are you doing? Barack Obama."

"I'm doing fine, sir. I'm your helicopter pilot, and I've got one up on Scott here . . . I'm actually a Marine."

Scott laughed at the jab, and Obama seemed to get it, too. "You know what? I can't wait to fly with you. I've never been in a helicopter before."

I looked him right in the eye, nodded, and said, "Sir, it was nice to meet you. And congratulations."

He said, "Thank you very much."

Biden was right behind him, observing all this, and then he shook our hands and said, "Good to meet you fellows."

And that was the first time I actually met my new Commander in Chief.

His first opportunity to fly came just a couple of weeks later. This was a significant event, and everyone wanted to be part of the first Presidential lift. Sergeant Williams and Sergeant Kish were my two senior crew chiefs, and they had flipped a coin to decide who would fly the Inauguration and who would fly this lift. Sergeant Kish had done the Inauguration, so now it was Sergeant Williams on the crew this morning.

We were only going to fly the President from the White House to marry up with *Air Force One* at Andrews, but it was a good chance for me to observe how the new administration played with others. Not unlike the transfer of power from President Bush 41 to President Clinton, HMX-1 was adjusting again to a new boss.

Because of my experiences during the transition from Bush 41 to Clinton, I assigned my staff to gather certain information. For instance, we sent in a request to Obama's staff about his family's preferences for snacks and beverages on *Marine One*. The staff was incredulous that we were asking this kind of stuff, because the President and First Lady were not yet accustomed to flying in an aircraft that catered to their wishes. They pretty much just asked for healthy snacks, juice and water, so we stocked the cabin with those items.

Not only did we reconfigure *Marine One* to suit the new President, but I remembered all too well the hubbub in the media when President Clinton had failed to salute the crew chief on his first *Marine One* flight. I knew that President Obama had no military experience, so I doubted that he would be familiar with our traditions and ceremonies.

I called my boss and said, "Sir, I'm willing to bet that nobody on the staff has thought to mention the protocol for saluting my crew chief. We don't want the whole world to see him botch it."

My boss agreed that it was a good idea, and said he would bring the issue up to the new staff. I later spoke about the issue to the military aide prior to the flight. He said, "Trust me, Frenchy, all five of us mil aides sat the boss down and gave him our guidance on how to board the aircraft properly. He's got it."

I was relieved to hear it, and glad to avoid another awkward moment and subsequent media blitz. We landed on the White House lawn exactly five minutes before the designated pickup time. I shut down the rotors, kept the engines running, and Sergeant Williams positioned the air stairs and waited for the President's arrival. Perfect timing.

Twenty minutes passed. I wasn't going to make judgment calls, but President Bush's staff was the most synchronized I had ever seen, and perhaps I had gotten spoiled by their consistent punctuality. President Clinton's staff had sometimes kept us waiting like this, but I just chalked it up to this being the first lift, and the new administration getting into a good rhythm.

As always, I had a backup aircraft positioned in the air nearby, just in case I need them. Due to fuel concerns, I eventually called the pilot on the radio and told him, "Night Hawk Two, head back to base and stand by. I will let you know when I'm airborne."

The President came out twenty-five minutes after we landed, and the cameras went crazy. There were also hundreds of people on the rope line, cheering and snapping their own pictures. I watched out the cockpit window as he approached the stairs.

Sergeant Williams threw his hand up in a snappy salute, and the President returned it perfectly. The military aide had also briefed him that he didn't need to talk to the Marine or anything like that, but he decided otherwise. After the salute, the President walked right up to Sergeant Williams and extended his hand. "How you doing? I'm President Obama."

I could only imagine what was going through Sergeant Williams's head as he stood there frozen in time for a moment. Dozens of cameras caught the moment, and Sergeant Williams had that surprised look in his eyes, as if to say, *Are you actually talking to me?*

I watched as he moved his hand from the salute position to shake the President's hand and exchange a few words. Next, the President climbed aboard and leaned into the cockpit. He shook my hand and my copilot's, and thanked us jokingly in advance for a smooth ride. He then went into the cabin and took his seat, and I imagined what it must be like to occupy the Presidential seat for the first time.

A few seconds later, Sergeant Williams entered the cockpit and sat down. He put on his headset, looked at me in distress, and said, "Sir, I am so sorry. I didn't know what to do. He just started talking to me."

Williams thought he was in trouble with me because he had broken the position of attention to shake the President's hand.

I looked at him and said, "Sergeant Williams, the President of the United States put his hand out and started talking to you. You did exactly what you were supposed to do. Forget about it. No big deal at all."

We brought the President over to Andrews, where he thanked us again before boarding *Air Force One*. Before I even got back to Anacostia, I was getting calls from the military aide: "Who was that Marine? Why was the President talking to him?"

I had to call my boss and explain to him what had happened, and why Sergeant Williams had broken protocol. The next day, of course, all this was televised. It provided a great newsreel, portraying President Obama taking time out to talk to a Marine as he was boarding *Marine One.* This kind of thing had not happened in a decade, so Sergeant Williams was the focus of a good deal of teasing, I'm sure, but everyone knew that he had done exactly the right thing.

•   •   •

Not long after that first lift, I flew the Obama family to Camp David for the first time. Again, this was a place I was intimately familiar with, so it was fascinating to imagine how the First Family would like it.

I was on the White House lawn at the right time, and out comes the President, the First Lady, her mother, and their two daughters. I knew who would be on the lift, so I had picked up a couple of HMX-1 models that were all the rage in our HMX-1 gift shop.

I had placed notes on all the seats, and for the girls, the notes were tucked under the helicopters. The note to the President and First Lady simply said, "Welcome aboard *Marine One*. We are looking forward to serving you. Colonel Frenchy L'Heureux."

The notes for the girls said, "Welcome, Malia and Sasha. We are happy to have you aboard. Colonel Frenchy L'Heureux."

When the family boarded, the President leaned in and said hello in his congenial manner. Mrs. Obama then stopped by the cockpit as well, and said, "Oh my gosh. This is my first helicopter ride. I am so excited!"

When I landed at Camp David, Mrs. Obama again stopped by and said, "Thank you so much for the toys, they are absolutely wonderful. The flight was beautiful, I just loved it."

She also had each of the girls come into the cockpit and say thank you, which was very sweet.

That weekend, there was no Peloton One. I did challenge some of the guys to a friendly game of walleyball, and some of them were later invited to play basketball with the President. I don't have an ounce of talent on the basketball court, so I passed on that one. This was going to be one of my last visits to Camp David, and I felt quite nostalgic as I tried to soak it all in. I was already training the next HMX-1 CO by this time, and over the next few months I began to let my other *Marine One* pilots handle more lifts as I prepared for my next assignment.

The Sixty-fifth Anniversary of D-day

My last mission with HMX-1 was one of the most historically significant events of my life. This time, I flew President Obama during the
sixty-fifth anniversary of D-day in Normandy. The last time I was here,
I had flown President Clinton as the WHLO for the fiftieth anniversary
of the event. I don't think very many Marines got a chance to do this
once, let alone twice. Now I was the CO, and would actually land the
President right at the cemetery. They did an "anniversary" every five
years or so, and this was probably one of the last ones in which any
WW II vets would still be alive.

Sergeant Kish was my crew chief on this trip, and just like the trip
to Germany and London, we broke down the VH-3s to fit them in the
back of a C-17. In the day preceding the event, we had to again fly the
ten hours after reassembling the VH-3s. First, we flew over the countryside a bit, then I took the crew up and down the coast, looking down at
places like Deauville, Caille, Isigny-sur-Mer, Red Beach, Gold Beach,
and Omaha Beach.

I was still stunned by what had happened on those beaches below
us. We could still see obstacles in the water, big craters in the ground,
and the gun emplacements in Pointe du Hoc. On the day of the ceremony, we landed *Marine One* and Night Hawk Two right there in
Colleville at the Normandy American Cemetary and Memorial, where
our war dead are buried. All of the other visiting heads of state had
to land in a field down below and then ride in a motorcade up to the
cemetery. But this is U.S. sovereign soil, so all eyes and cameras were
on us when we landed.

The President left the aircraft and participated in a summit with
other world leaders. Next, there was a long ceremony with lots of
speakers. We had free access to the area, so we walked around and
took in the sights. Steven Spielberg and Tom Hanks, the guys who
brought us *Saving Private Ryan*, were in the crowd.

After the day's events, we flew the President back to the airfield and began preparing for the journey home. We were good at this, and everything was smooth and synchronized. Now we broke down the VH-3s again and walked up the back ramp of the C-17.

For most of the guys, it was just another ride home. But it was especially poignant for me, since I knew it would be my last. I spent some time in quiet reflection, looking around me and thinking about everything I had been privileged to do with this outstanding organization.

CHAPTER 9

MARINE ONE, OUT

I had flown the Obama family around the United States, to Camp David, and to France, watching them settle into their new lives. Now it was my turn to say goodbye. Six months into President Obama's tenure, I handed over the reins of my beloved HMX-1 to the next Commander. Colonel Jerry Glavy would become the twenty-third HMX-1 Commander.

My change-of-command ceremony took place on June 19, 2009. This was the height of HMX-1 ceremony and tradition, and there were more than five hundred people in attendance. We were actually on the flight line at Quantico, which had been closed down for the event. Distinguished guests were seated under a special tent in the middle of it all. I watched with everyone else as the white tops came in, smooth and shining in the bright afternoon sun. Most of the HMX-1 workforce was standing in a traditional formation, and with the white tops prestaged among them, they became part of a gorgeous and powerful panorama of machines and Marines.

After several people from the squadron made some remarks, after my wife and the new HMX-1 Commander's wife were presented with bouquets of roses, and after the band and Color Guard performed several songs and movements, the event narrator read a letter from President Bush and another from President Obama. Finally, I was introduced.

I walked up to the predetermined spot and turned around to face the crowd. I had done so many things and met so many interesting characters along the way, and here were many of them, smiling back at me, waiting to hear what I would say. Talk about full circle. Standing there before my mentors, family, and friends, with the white tops and all my Marines in formation behind me, everything felt just right. I could still remember that flying lesson as a kid.

I took a breath and gave my speech, which I had thought about in the days and weeks before, but which I chose to do without notes, and from the heart. My parents were there, and their pride was palpable. They had supported me so much. And from seeing Camp David and *Marine One* and Crawford and everything else vicariously through my excited phone calls and visits home, to visiting the Oval Office and attending military ceremonies like this one, my parents had enjoyed a front-row seat to the incredible career they made possible.

During the speech I thanked Dianna for her strength and love and support, and mentioned my kids, Delia and Ray Jr., who were sitting right next to her. I shared with the guests how my "kids" were now a lawyer and a Marine Officer, and how I couldn't have been more proud. Steve, Bayou, and Spanky were there, and I smiled over at them when I mentioned all the people who had shared this incredible journey with me. I thanked a lot of other people, congratulated Colonel Glavy, and made special mention of my mentors. Ned and Willie were sitting right there among them.

But most of all, I spoke about how much I loved the dedicated people standing behind me in formation. I ended with a quote from Ronald Reagan: "We got something pretty good. We made it a little better. We're leaving it in good hands. Overall, not bad."

I had two more assignments and posts after HMX-1, working with some of the finest men and women you can imagine. My predecessor at HMX-1 once said, "We are not a bunch of special Marines do an average mission. We are a bunch of average Marines doing a very special mission." I could not have agreed more. Knowing that nothing could ever top my incredible experiences as CO of HMX-1, I decided to end my career in the Marine Corps in 2011, after three decades of service.

Looking Back

In the five decades that HMX-1 has been transporting the President of the United States, I was the twenty-second Commanding Officer. One hundred years from now, I'll be one of the faces looking out from a nice frame in the HMX-1 hallway or museum. Because of the timing of my tours, I straddled two administrations each time and experienced the transition of power. I also got to fly the last two Presidents of the twentieth century and the first two of the twenty-first. Likewise, I flew the first Presidential Inauguration and victory lap of the twenty-first century. My parents, family, friends, and thousands of fellow Marines were right there with me the whole time. Since my family lived near Quantico during my HMX-1 tours, there were even a couple of times when I got to fly *Marine One* over my house, and look down at my own kids waving. Wow.

I was the first person in my family to join the Marine Corps, and the military. When I joined, I had no idea where it would take me. What began as a young college student's plan to become a pilot became a thirty-year adventure, and the greatest honor of my life. The Marine Corps gave me the opportunity to travel to numerous countries and multiple continents, and to see most of it from the cockpit of a helicopter. I can't say enough about all the incredible men and women I worked with there, and in all of my positions.

I was assigned to Hawaii for much of my career, which led to my decision to live here after leaving the Marines. I am now serving as the Assistant Superintendent of the Office of School Facilities and Support Services for the Hawaii Department of Education, in which both of my children finished their high school educations. While we have a very different mission, the complexity of my job is not much different than that of HMX-1. I've been trained and expected to create results in dynamic working conditions, and those skill sets still apply to my work today. Instead of helicopters and Marines and world leaders, I now interact with educators, school leadership, and state-government officials to manage the security and operations of hundreds of facilities.

While I was in the Marine Corps, I never looked back. I was too engaged in the work I was doing to focus on the past. As I write this, I've been out for a couple of years, and I can reflect with hindsight on all the lessons the Marine Corps taught me. Perhaps the most fundamental lessons I learned in thirty years are that leadership is a contact sport and that you must be willing to get your hands dirty. In the leadership positions I was selected for, I could not be afraid to make decisions. But, as with any human behavior, be it personal or professional, sometimes you make a decision and wish you had a do-over. In the Marines, you don't get many do-overs. You just take full responsibility for your actions, take accountability for the entire team, and continuously learn and grow from mistakes and successes alike.

I remember the feeling when I first took over HMX-1. It was the pinnacle of my career, and I knew it, and all I had to rely on with regard to handling that level of responsibility and the scope of that job was my experience as the Commanding Officer of HMH-362 (the Ugly Angels). During that role, I had been a very hands-on Commanding Officer, engaging with the workforce at every level of the squadron. Ultimately, I was able to hone the workforce into a dynamic and cohesive unit with a shared vision. The patches we wore on our flight suits became emblems of our deep sense of collective pride and devotion to the organization and to one another.

I was told that I would not be able to lead HMX-1 in the same way. It was just too big, and there were too many moving parts. After a career of learning as much as I could from my former Commanders and mentors, and then from my own Command experience, I disagreed. One of the things I learned as CO of HMH-362 was that I had a gift for learning and being able to recall a Marine's name. This may not seem like much, or be viewed as important to the casual observer. But to that young Marine, that Lance Corporal walking across the hangar deck, it means something. He might feel like he is so far down on the totem pole that his presence in the squadron is unremarkable. Then, the "boss" addresses him by his earned rank and name, recalls his home state, and initiates a conversation about his work in the squadron, and that young Marine realizes that his CO knows exactly who he is and is actually *thanking* him for his efforts!

HMX-1 was seven times the size of HMH-362, but I made it a point to learn the name and personal information of every single member of the unit. Among many other forms of leadership, this helped me to propel HMX-1's overall morale and esprit de corps through the roof. For example, as in any job or task I was given, I always strove to do the right thing, to put Marines first and mission second. Such a culture breeds success. Of course, HMX-1 was a bit more kinetic than most organizations, and the mission so visible that it really did consume most daily interactions and decision making. There was no room for human or mechanical incompetence, and every facet of operations had to be flawless. I was awestruck by the professionalism and dedication of the men and women who made it all possible.

I served in amazing organizations with incredible people, and HMX-1 is the most professional, most beloved organization of them all. I don't know what would've happened if somehow I had botched a landing, put the President in danger, or, God forbid, crashed *Marine*

One. I like to think that my Marines, and the incredible support system of HMX-1, would have understood that these things do happen. But deep down where it really counts, I put more pressure on myself than anyone else ever could.

Another one of my most cherished memories and experiences, and the opportunity of a lifetime, was the relationship I was able to have with President Bush. Even though my job required me to take a very nonpolitical approach to the President, whoever he may be, I still got to see the personal side of President Bush. In between all the missions, logistics, and planning, I rode bikes with him and helped with the trail at Crawford. And in doing so, I couldn't help but begin to see him as a regular guy. Of course, I did not forget that the regular guy was also the President of the United States, but I still marveled at the privilege of getting to know him on that level. I never once took it for granted, and I was giddy as a kid about every bike ride or conversation that took place.

I have kept in touch with President Bush, exchanging Christmas cards each year. In April 2013, I received an invitation to the dedication ceremony for the George W. Bush Presidential Library and Museum. When Presidents Bush 41, Bush 43, Clinton, and Carter stood on the stage with their wives, I was sitting in the audience, and realized that I had flown almost everyone up there.

At the prededication dinner the night before the ceremony, the President was just as I remembered him—a man with the energy of a teenager, a comic's sense of humor and timing, and a serious set of lungs and legs that could propel him on the trails with speed and stamina. Despite having one of the most intense jobs in the world, and dealing with a plethora of national issues, I always found President Bush down-to-earth, kind, and selfless. I feel very lucky to have served as his pilot and to call him a friend. He even told me that the invitation to come back to ride the trail at Crawford still stands.

●　　●　　●

So many things have changed, but some remain the same. I still see Marine helicopters flying around Hawaii all the time. I still run on the beaches and compete in local triathlons. I still scan the horizon for weather on my drive into the office, as if I were going to fly the Boss that day. I also have nine helicopter models that sit on a shelf in my office now. When I was a kid, those models hanging from the ceiling of my bedroom represented a hopeful career in aviation. The ones that sit before me now are daily reminders of the wonderful career I've had.

Someone once wrote, "Every man's memory is his own private literature." I don't think I could possibly be more grateful or humbled by my own collection.

ACKNOWLEDGMENTS

There are so many people I could thank, because without them these stories, these memories, and this book would not have been possible. I would like to thank all of the Marines, Sailors, and civilians I have served with, and those still serving. There are personalities with names like Paco, Quarters, Spanky, Bayou, Skippy, and Cajun—aviators all. And those venerable and salty Crew Chiefs—if not for them, I am quite sure I would never have become the pilot and leader I was entrusted to be. In dark nights and choppy seas, tight landing zones and unstable suspended loads . . . they did the real work.

I would also like to thank some of my mentors, including Lieutenant Colonel Richard "Willie" Willard, Lieutenant Colonel Ned Paulson, Admiral Tom Fargo, and Lieutenant General Keith Stalder. You are all incredible patriots, mentors, and friends.

Finally, I would like to personally thank President George W. Bush for introducing me to the thrill of mountain biking, and for the unforgettable rides. As the President once said to me after a particularly brutal day on the trails: "If you're not bleeding, you're not riding!"

INDEX